FREEDOM:

Escape Negativity & Overthinking to Live Happily & Find Your Purpose

COPYRIGHT

FREE GIFT

Greetings!

First of all, I want to thank you for reading my books. I aim to create the very best books for my readers.

Now I invite you to join my exclusive list. As a subscriber, you will receive a free gift, weekly tips, free giveaways, discounts, and so much more.

All of this is 100% free with no strings attached.

To claim your bonus, simply head to the link below or scan the QR code.

---

https://www.subscribepage. com/swindali

CONTENTS

INTRODUCTION

Are you in control of your life? I know it's a weird question to ask, because you're the one who makes the decisions around here, right? But does it really feel like you're in control of your life? Or do you find yourself not living the way you expected to? Maybe you have regrets about the past and wish you could go back in time. Or there were times when you wish you had said something else. Maybe you're constantly frustrated, overwhelmed, and anxious about the future—thinking about all the things that might go wrong and how embarrassing it would be for you.

I have felt all of that many times. I know how thoughts can be overwhelming. Those same thoughts get stuck in your head. Weeks, months, and sometimes years pass by. Still, you just can't stop those thoughts. One day they make you feel a certain way, and the next day it's like you've done a full turnaround and gone the other way.

Just like me, you've probably found yourself holding back in conversations because you worry about what other people will think. Or maybe you avoid doing something because it seems too complicated. Maybe you often compare yourself to other people. You see how they are living their best life whilst yours sucks. Why can't my life be like theirs? What's wrong with me? You lie awake at night thinking the same, repetitive thoughts.

How did it all go wrong? You stare at the ceiling in the darkness, worrying about something bad that might happen to you. Making a decision feels too hard. Getting over what happened feels impossible.

On and on the overthinking goes...

Overthinking is defined as excessive thinking that has no benefit. The process of overthinking can make decision-making and life in general much more difficult. Not only does it cloud your mental capabilities, but it can also have serious negative consequences on your well-being. Research has found that overthinkers struggle with sleep, emotional distress, and many other issues. Often, they try to escape that distress through unhealthy coping strategies, such as alcohol or other vices.

Escapism

A report in the *Journal of Abnormal Psychology* shared that 52% of people between 45 and 55 years old say they overthink. Overthinking is also linked with mental health problems such as anxiety, depression, and OCD (Obsessive-Compulsive Disorder). The National Institute of Mental Health says that over 30% of adults in the U.S. will face an anxiety disorder at some time, often as a result of overthinking. And it is a vicious cycle. As overthinkers think more and more about their problems, the more complicated they seem to become. More problems arise, which leads to increased stress and emotional turmoil. To escape their mental trauma, many abuse alcohol or indulge in other vices. Although those vices might help us to escape in the short term and give us a brief hit of pleasure, the aftermath is usually one of regret and pain.

Adding to the complications of overthinking are the distractions, manipulation, and influence we face on a daily basis. Never before has life been so chaotic. Choosing what to wear, what to eat, what to listen to, who to date becomes exhausting.

It's great to have unlimited choices, but they can also make life more complicated. We're assailed by distracting thoughts and content and targeted manipulation in all forms. It all comes at a cost. Often the cost is mental health. Choice and distractions can overwhelm us if we allow them to. On the other hand, they can allow us to be the best version of ourselves. Knowing how the key is.

Overthinking consumes a lot of energy. Energy that is not being used productively. Energy that could be used to improve your life. Overthinking things is not logical, rational, reasonable, or normal behavior. As a result, we easily make mistakes and lack direction. It's like being stuck in a storm at sea with no visible way out. Finding our way is the route to purpose, meaning, and clarity.

Like many others, I have faced the struggles of

finding purpose, making decisions, and getting lost in overthinking. When I was growing up, my mind seemed to be surrounded by dark clouds. My childhood was pretty crazy, and I'm sure that influenced the darkness. I had an older brother who was heavily addicted to drugs. He was constantly in and out of jail. Seeing this was very confusing for me. After all, he was my older brother and I looked up to him. Each day there was a new drama, and it caused a lot of chaos in my family. Unfortunately, it all ended badly. He tried to improve, but one day he was late for an appointment and stole a car. The police chased after him. Driving recklessly, he tried to escape but sadly was killed in a collision.

For a long time after that, the dark clouds weighed heavily on my thoughts. I just couldn't see through it all. I couldn't make sense of my thoughts. For many years, I drifted without any purpose, direction, or fulfillment in my life. There were wasted years, dead-end jobs, dissatisfaction, and confusion in my head. Things changed at a certain point when I stopped being a victim. When I chose to take responsibility for my thoughts and decided I was going to do something about them.

Over the last few years, studying and my real-life experiences have uncovered a ton of value regarding finding purpose, making decisions, and overthinking. In this book, I'm going to outline my personal experiences, scientific research, anecdotes, tools, methods, and tips to help you. These are the very things that have helped me to improve when I was going through tough times and couldn't see a way out. When I was faced with difficult decisions. When I lacked direction, motivation, and purpose. What you will find in this book is what I needed the most.

Follow me out of the darkness.

CHALLENGE 1

In each chapter of this book, there will be a challenge. Some are written. Write in this book or your own notepad. If you're reading on a device, then use a digital notepad. Either is fine. Just make sure you **do the work.**

At the top of the page, I want you to answer the following questions.

- *How has overthinking held me back in my life?*

____

____

____

____

- *Over the last few months, what has been my biggest worry?*

____

____

____

- *Over the last few months, what has been my biggest regret?*

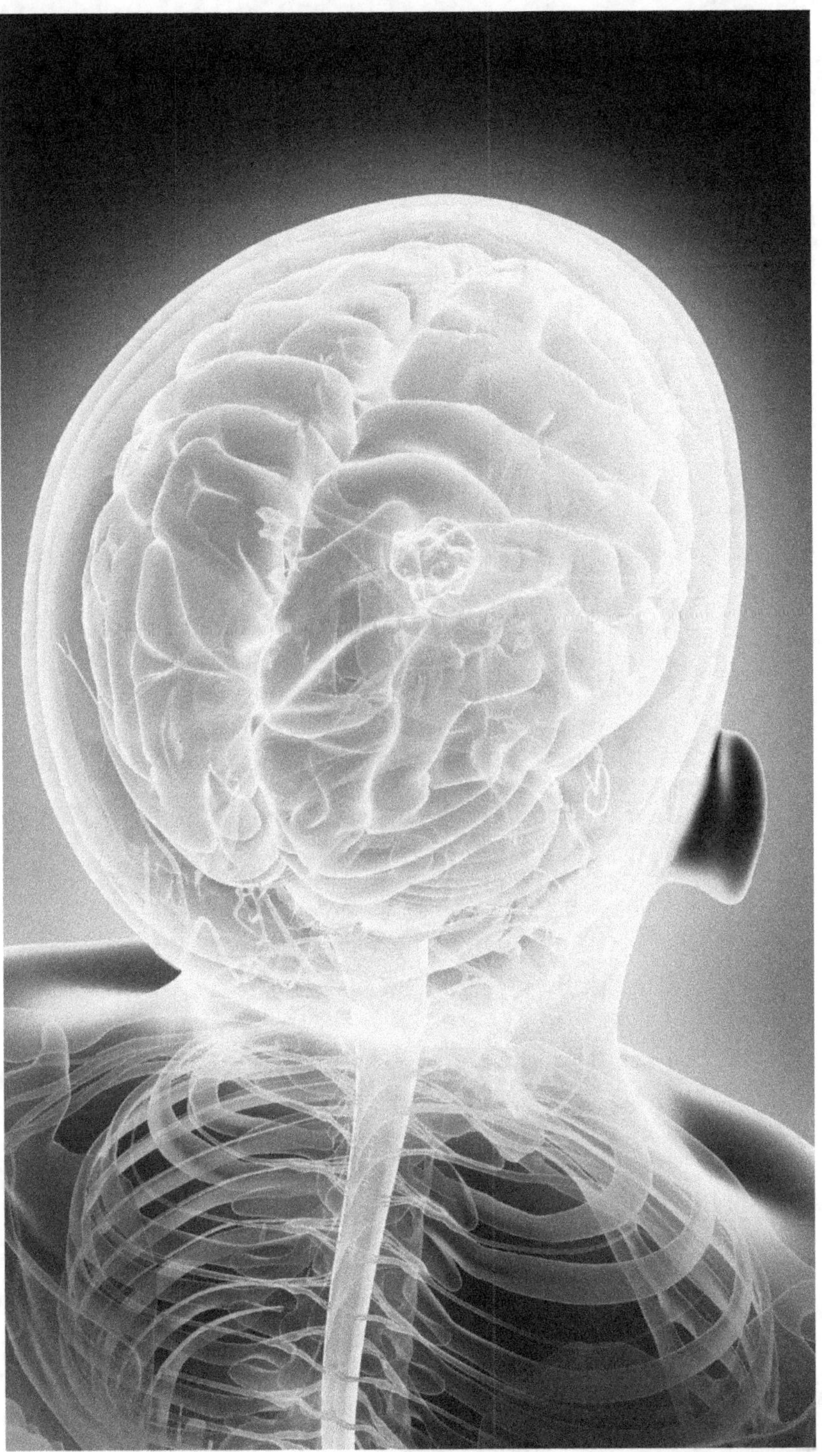

CHAPTER 1
WHY CHANGE IS HARD

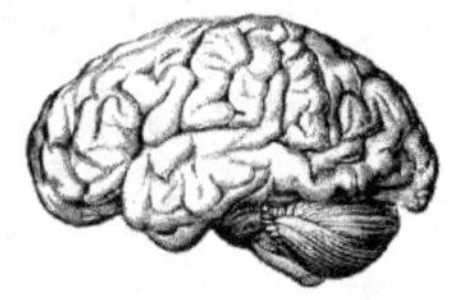

The movie *A Beautiful Mind* (2001) tells the story of John Nash, a brilliant mathematician who struggles with schizophrenia. It shows how intense intellectual activity, combined with his condition, leads to overthinking. Nash's struggle to distinguish his delusions from reality can be seen as an extreme form of overthinking, where his mind constantly creates patterns and connections that don't exist.

Like Nash, we might think that overthinking will lead us somewhere useful. However, it usually disrupts our minds and makes it difficult to move forward in a positive way. But we need to think, right? After all, it's what sets us apart from animals. Einstein thought about the theory of relativity. Darwin's thoughts revealed the nature of the species. Elon Musk thinks about rockets, electric cars, and businesses that make billions of dollars. Taylor Swift thinks of melodies. Thoughts are powerful indeed.

What will be discussed in this book is the kind of overthinking that is not helpful. The repetitive, anxious, and overall unproductive thoughts. If you're reading this book, you probably know what I'm talking about. Those times when overthinking clouds your judgment and you can't think clearly. When you get lost in thoughts that go nowhere or that push you backward. When you get stuck on the negatives or lost in the worst-case scenario. By understanding how our brains work and identifying unhelpful thought patterns, we can work on replacing them with more constructive ones or finding peace. We can then make better decisions, find purpose, and live a higher-quality life.

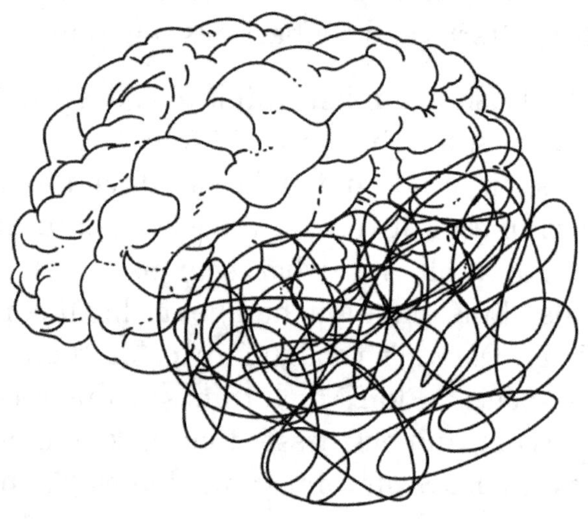

Human nature

We humans like to think of ourselves as logical, but it's not quite so simple. Fundamentally, we are led by our biology and emotions. Deterministic theories say it's our fate. That we don't have free will because our biology has already decided the outcome. Naturally, that often causes us to make bad decisions due to inherent biases that can work against us.

Humans may have been around for thousands of years, but our brains are still wired on old circuitry. For the majority of human history, we have lived in a very different environment from the one in which we now live. It's only within the last hundred or so years that we have arrived at a modern and comfortable standard of living. Not so long ago, we had to face the constant threat of death. Mental shortcuts in our brain helped us to make quick-fire decisions that could save us. Those are still triggered today, but the circumstances of modern life are quite different.

Our brains have evolved sophisticated mechanisms to ensure our survival, responding swiftly to immediate threats such as predatory animals or the challenges of tribal life. This evolutionary journey has led to the development of key brain chemicals that regulate our responses to various situations. Dopamine, for instance, motivates us to act by promising a reward once we overcome a problem, initiating a loop of problem-solving thought processes. Adrenaline then provides the energy needed to persist in these efforts. As we explore potential solutions, serotonin contributes to our sense of well-being, encouraging our continued engagement. However, when solutions elude us, our serotonin levels can fall, leading to an increase in cortisol and a subsequent rise in stress. This cycle can trap us in a state of overthinking as we struggle to find a way out of the problem at hand.

Environment

Human nature is one side of overthinking, but our external environments also contribute to it. Consider the story of Alex, a young student caught in the whirlwind of academic expectations. From a young age, he was raised with the belief that excellence in school was the golden ticket to a successful life. This belief, deeply ingrained, turned every assignment into a heavy task and filled him with anxiety and self-doubt.

One evening, he sat at his desk, staring at a mathematics problem that, under different circumstances, might have taken a few minutes to solve. Hours passed by and the page remained mostly blank, save for a few tentative marks. It wasn't the complexity of the problem that held Alex back but the weight of the belief that his entire future hinged on the perfection of his academic work. This single homework assignment morphed in his mind into a make-or-break moment for his academic career.

Alex's overthinking was not an isolated phenomenon but a symptom of the broader cultural and societal expectations surrounding academic achievement. The narrative of needing to excel creates an environment ripe for overthinking. Students are a prime example of this culture, often finding themselves comparing their achievements to those of their peers. They worry incessantly about upcoming exams, fearing any mistake, no matter how minor, as a potential derailment of their path to success.

This pressure cooker of expectations does not just cultivate overthinking; it fosters an environment in which stress and anxiety thrive, overshadowing the joys of learning and exploration. The balance between striving for excellence and maintaining mental well-being becomes increasingly skewed, leading to a life where academic pursuits overshadow personal growth and happiness.

The tale of Alex and countless others like him underscores the critical need for a cultural shift: a reevaluation of what we value and celebrate in the journey of learning and development. It highlights the importance of nurturing environments that emphasize balance, well-being, and the understanding that one's worth is not solely determined by accolades but by the richness of one's experiences and the depth of one's character. In achieving this, we can begin to untangle the knot of overthinking and gain a healthy perspective on success and failure.

Homeostasis

The journey through the challenges of overthinking, illustrated by the experiences of individuals such as John Nash and countless other students burdened by academic pressures, points to a deeper, underlying mechanism at play. Just as our bodies instinctively strive for equilibrium, our minds engage in a similar quest for balance. This quest, however, is complicated by the barrage of information, expectations, and decisions we face daily, all of which lead to the mental gridlock we recognize as overthinking.

Homeostasis is inherent in human beings. It is the process of self-regulation by which an organism adjusts to survive. In humans, it's like an automatic control system that ensures we function properly. The process includes maintaining body temperature, pH levels, and hydration. Overall, it's crucial for health, and if disrupted, it can lead to illnesses. In the context of personal development, homeostasis acts as a natural resistance to change. Essentially, your body and mind want to keep things as they are. When you try to make a change, such as starting a new exercise routine, changing your diet, or starting a new habit, your body and mind will resist. They want to stay with the old ways because they want to keep us stable and safe. Of course, there's some good in that. However, if we want to improve ourselves, we have to face challenges.

Picture life as a climb up a steep slope. The steeper the slope, the greater the challenge. Without continuous effort, you risk sliding back down. This dynamic reflects the principle of homeostasis, which maintains our stability and safety but can also keep us from progressing. As our bodies age and the world evolves, pushing against this natural resistance becomes essential for growth. Essentially, progress involves signaling to both your body and your mind that you are in command. Although mastering this balance of applying pressure and adapting to change is challenging initially, it becomes more manageable with practice and persistence. The question is are you ready to make a change? Or are you addicted to overthinking because losing yourself in thoughts is an escape from reality?

An ancient sage once said, "When the student

is ready, the teacher will appear."

And if *you* are ready to make a change, then keep on reading.

CHALLENGE 2

In the last chapter, we learned how our biology and environment can sometimes hold us back. Think about the ways in which you or your environment are holding you back. First, let's look at how you might be holding yourself back.

Bad habit tracker

Do you have any bad habits? Are these a way of escaping from overthinking?

Identify one bad habit you have. Put a mark on your calendar when you last did that. Try to increase the time until when you do it again. When you slip off and fall into it, make a log of why. Find out what your triggers are and replace them with something better.

____

____

____

____

Environment

Think about how your environment is holding

you back. It could be something simple such as the place you work, where you live, or your social circle. What are you going to do about it? What small action can you take today to start the ball rolling in the correct direction?

____

____

____

____

____

____

____

CHAPTER 2
FALSE REALITY

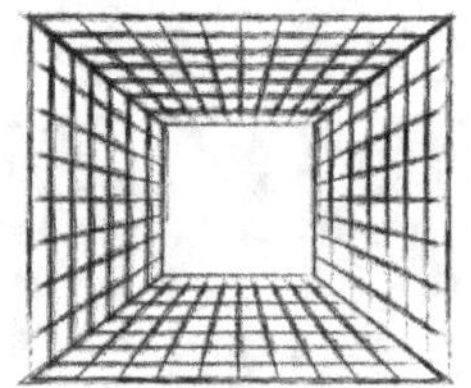

Once upon a time, in the small village of Cottingley, England, lived two young cousins named Elsie Wright and Frances Griffiths. In the summer of 1917, amidst the shadows of World War I, they embarked on an adventure that would stir the imaginations of people around the world.

Elsie and Frances captured a series of photographs that would become known as the Cottingley Fairies. These images, five in total, depicted the girls in their garden, seemingly interacting with fairies dancing in the air. At first glance, these photographs were a marvel, a glimpse into a magical world that many wished to believe existed alongside our own.

The story of these photographs spread far and wide, eventually capturing the attention of Sir Arthur Conan Doyle, the famous author known for his tales about Sherlock Holmes. Doyle, a spiritualist at heart, was enchanted by the images. He saw in them proof of the supernatural. He used the photographs to illustrate articles for a magazine and later in a book, further propelling the fame of the Cottingley Fairies.

The public was divided, caught between skepticism and wonder. Many were eager to grasp at the possibility of a magical escape from the grim realities of their times. Spiritualism was on the rise, and the Cottingley Fairies became a symbol of hope, a testament to the belief in something beyond the tangible.

For decades, the true nature of the photographs remained a mystery, fueling speculation and investigation. It was a puzzle that many attempted to solve, with theories and explanations swirling around the origins of the fairies. However, it wasn't until the 1980s that the truth was revealed by the now-elderly Elsie and Frances. They confessed that the fairies were not ethereal beings, but rather clever fabrications made from cardboard cutouts. By using hatpins to stand the cutouts in the ground, they had created an enchanting illusion of dancing fairies.

The tale of the Cottingley Fairies is a poignant reminder of the human capacity for belief and the power of imagination to create wonders. It also serves as an early lesson in manipulation. Nowadays, manipulation is everywhere in our world, from personal relationships to the media we face on a daily basis. And as an overthinker, you might very well be a prime victim of it.

Influence

"According to a study by Dr Martin Hilbert at the University of Southern California, in 2007, Americans consumed information for almost 12 hours per day. (

Influence is a high-yield economy. All day long, people, companies, and life are trying to influence, manipulate, and persuade you. The news, in particular, influences public opinion by playing on our emotions. It gets views because it triggers primal states such as fear, anger, and loss. Those are powerful emotions that create opinions, moods, and beliefs. All of this stacks up into our subconscious and gives us a distorted view of the world. Statistically, however, many of those events are very small in probability. The news sensationalizes and sometimes fakes things. Ultimately, it can cause us to overthink and build an unrealistic view of the world.

It's not just the news, either. You must be aware of all forms of content that you engage with. Consider what kind of YouTube videos, social media, movies, and music you consume. There is infinite negativity in the world these days. If we let it into our lives, it can derail us. Understand that it is all influencing you, building up your beliefs and manifesting them into reality. Sure, those sad songs may bring back memories of a lost love, but maybe it's time to move on. And it's nice to know what's going on in the world, but does it have an influence on the grander scheme of your life or is it taking away from you?

Uncertainty

Manipulation creates uncertainty, and that is something the human mind doesn't like. The mind seeks familiarity. When it's faced with uncertainty, it spirals into overthinking about all the what-ifs and various scenarios. This seldom leads to any concrete conclusions. As a result, the overthinker becomes stuck in a loop without any closure.

Overthinking causes us to question, doubt, and criticize ourselves. This is how an interrogator probes for information. Our mind begins using tactics such as those used in military interrogation where the manipulation of emotions leads the subject to question or doubt themselves. Military interrogation techniques are designed to destabilize an individual in order to extract information. Techniques such as presenting false narratives, exploiting fears, and creating helplessness are not confined to those interrogation rooms. When we recognize this parallel, we can see our overthinking not just as a bad habit but as a form of our own mental manipulation.

For an overthinker, all this internal dialogue becomes a form of self-manipulation: the mind thinks it has certainty and control, but it ends up creating more uncertainty and distress. We become prisoners of our own minds and get trapped in false realities. False realities are often based on worst-case scenarios, unfounded worries, and a distorted perception of reality. We must understand this dynamic and question the validity of our repetitive thoughts. When we recognize that our overthinking is a form of our own manipulation, it can empower us to step back and critically evaluate the thoughts that are holding us hostage. This allows us to reclaim control over our thoughts and become mentally healthier and more balanced.

"Although you are not being brainwashed in

a lab nor dodging bullets, you do navigate a storm of advertising, nudges, biased news articles and propaganda."

A strong need for closure can foster decisiveness and clarity. It simplifies the world around us, making it easier to take action and commit to decisions. Commitment, whether to ideas, groups, or relationships, is foundational to human achievement. It instills a sense of loyalty and stability that is vital for any lasting endeavor. Without this commitment, we risk being perpetually lost in a sea of options, unable to choose a path forward. However, this commitment might be at the expense of missing out on opportunities that ambiguity and patience may bring. In simple terms, such stability and familiarity might feel boring.

Open-mindedness, though, carries its own set of challenges when taken to an extreme. The pursuit of novelty and avoidance of certainty can lead to a lack of focus and a failure to build or maintain anything of lasting value. I'm sure you know all too well the discomfort of certainty and the fear around decision-making. In trying to escape, you might distract yourself with nonsense or with things that seem important, such as creating drama that doesn't really need to exist. All of that is a form of avoidance, and it's often avoiding the important underlying issues. While being open to new ideas and experiences enriches our lives, excessive openness may prevent us from developing deep, meaningful connections and achieving something worthwhile. It's this incessant search for the new that can detract from the satisfaction and sense of accomplishment that comes from dedication and perseverance.

In Arie Kruglanski's *Uncertain*, he suggests that the key to successfully managing our relationship with uncertainty lies in finding the "golden mean"—a state of balance between the extremes of closed-mindedness and open-mindedness. This middle path allows us to embrace the benefits of both perspectives: the decisiveness and commitment from a certain level of cognitive closure and the flexibility and growth that come from being open to new experiences. By striving for this equilibrium, we equip ourselves to make more nuanced decisions, fostering a life that is both stable and enriched by the diverse opportunities that uncertainty brings.

Ultimately, it is about enriching our life experiences. By confronting our default reactions to uncertainty, we can start to make better decisions that align with our goals and values. We don't necessarily have to eliminate uncertainty from our lives, but we can learn from it and navigate through it in better ways. This will open us to more possibilities, growth, resilience, and a deeper understanding of the world and ourselves.

Here are some techniques to help you:

- **Get the facts**: Overthinkers usually get lost in playing out all possible scenarios. Collect the factual evidence rather than speculating.
- **Emotional regulation**: One must learn to manage one's emotional responses rather than getting carried away by negative emotions. Ground yourself.
- **Strengthen your resilience**: Build psychological resilience and keep working on your inner self, using what I will teach you in this book.

Biases

Now it's not just the media. Our brain loves shortcuts, and they can be used to manipulate us as well. Our biases break down our complex world through time-saving mental shortcuts. Being aware of these shortcuts is important to negate overthinking or the rationality that causes us to make the wrong move. Here are some of our own internal biases to be aware of.

- **Social conformity**: Peer pressure can lead us in a negative or a positive direction. For example, when a restaurant is full, you'll be more likely to be curious about it and go in than if it's empty. The more people who follow an idea, the truer it appears. Social proof causes disruption in stocks, sales, social behavior, and much more.

- **The Dunning-Kruger effect**: This occurs when people overestimate their understanding or expertise. The crux of this issue lies in the assumption that being intelligent or knowledgeable in some areas means one cannot be wrong in others. This misjudgment leads to an overconfidence in their grasp of the subject, making them more vulnerable to accepting and propagating ideas that lack scientific or logical foundation. Sometimes we might misuse our intellect to "rationalize bizarre thoughts and harmful behaviors."

- **Anecdotal influence**: People often give undue weight to anecdotes, leading them to ignore broader statistical realities or base rates. For example, the news sometimes sensationalizes events that are very low in probability. Or we hear of someone becoming a rock star so we think we can. As a result, people may overestimate their chances of succeeding. Worse still, they may not even try.

- **Confirmation bias**: Have you ever been so sure of something that you just went ahead? Even when others warned you not to. This is likely confirmation bias in action. It is the tendency of humans to focus on what supports our views and ignore what doesn't. Inherently, this is a blind spot. As we become more convinced, we ignore contrary evidence. Even the bright red flags!

- **Projection:** Projection is a psychological defense mechanism where a person subconsciously denies their own attributes, thoughts, or emotions and ascribes them to others. Here's a simple way to think about it: Imagine you have a flashlight that shines a light on whatever you're thinking or feeling, but instead of pointing it at yourself, you point it at your friends. When you're feeling dishonest, instead of recognizing this trait in yourself, you "shine the light" on your friends, seeing dishonesty in them instead.

- **The sunk cost fallacy**: The sunk cost fallacy is our tendency to keep doing something due to our previous investments, even though it might be heading in the wrong direction. The fear of losing something has a stronger motivational effect than the possibility of gaining something of similar value. The pain of losing $100 is greater than the joy of finding $100. When we worry about the money or time we've already spent, it can be tough to make smart choices. We often feel stuck with our past decisions because we don't want to waste what we've invested, even when those decisions aren't helping us anymore.

Being aware of these biases is like having a compass in hand. It doesn't eliminate the obstacles but empowers us to navigate with greater awareness and care. By understanding our cognitive biases, we can chart a course toward more informed, balanced, and fulfilling decisions.

However, just being aware of them does not always stop them from working against us. Understanding that awareness alone doesn't inoculate us against biases, we must adopt strategies that enhance our critical thinking and decision-making processes. Here are several strategies aimed at achieving this:

- **Questioning**: Encourage an environment of skepticism and inquiry where assumptions are questioned and evidence is evaluated critically.

- **Diverse perspectives**: Actively seek out diverse viewpoints and information sources. Constructive criticism from others can provide external checks on our biases and assumptions. Encourage feedback that is openly given and received.

- **Structured decision-making**: Employ decision-making frameworks that ensure thorough analysis. Tools such as checklists, pros and cons lists, and decision matrices can help in systematically evaluating options, reducing the likelihood of oversights due to cognitive shortcuts. More on this later.

- **Reflection and self-awareness**: Cultivate a practice of reflecting on one's thought processes and decisions. Recognizing when and how biases influence our thinking can be the first step in counteracting them. Developing mindfulness can help in recognizing the emotional reactions that often accompany and reinforce biases. By managing our emotions, we can make more rational decisions.

- **Collaborative decision-making**: Engage in group decision-making processes where possible. A group of diverse individuals can bring multiple perspectives to the table, helping to counteract individual biases.

By integrating the strategies outlined in this chapter, we can fortify ourselves against the inherent biases that our mental shortcuts often lead us toward. These cognitive shortcuts, while sometimes helpful, can also make us susceptible to the kinds of enchantments and illusions that led even the wise mind of Sir Arthur Conan Doyle astray in the case of the Cottingley Fairies.

The strategies we've begun to explore, from having a questioning mind to diversifying our perspectives, lay the groundwork for a more resilient, informed approach to navigating the world around us. A world increasingly filled with complex information and persuasive narratives designed to influence our thoughts and actions.

In the chapters that follow, we will delve even deeper into practical methods for sharpening your instincts and enhancing your decision-making capabilities. We'll explore how to apply these strategies in real-world scenarios, ensuring that your brain's desire for shortcuts doesn't lead you astray. Instead, you will learn to navigate these challenges with a critical eye, preserving your sense of wonder while grounding your beliefs in reality.

CHALLENGE 3

Pay attention to the content you consume. For one week, put some trackers on your laptop and phone. Look at your watch history. Make notes on all of it. Ask yourself about what you consume.

- *Is it negative?*

____

____

____

____

- *Is it uplifting?*

____

____

____

____

- *Is it helping me?*

40

CHAPTER 3
LIVING IN DARKNESS

What are these thoughts?

I was seated on a bus driving through rugged mountains and dense jungles to a faraway beach destination. In anticipation of the fifteen-hour bus journey, I had downloaded some audio files to my phone. I plugged in my wired earphones, and on a long, dark bus journey, a light slowly came on in my mind.

In the darkness, I played an audiobook and listened as an eccentric man talked about how, one night, he had become aware of his thoughts. He told how he had spent two years sitting on park benches "in the moment." Interspersed by bell sounds, it was as if this man was reading my mind. How did he know I had a voice in there? How did he know what it was saying? Suddenly, I realized I wasn't the only one who had dark and confusing thoughts. Moreover, I realized that my thoughts don't define me.

That long bus journey gave me a glimmer of hope, breaking through the dark clouds of my mind. I listened to that whole audiobook in one go. It was *The Power of Now* by Eckhart Tolle. It was a revelation about "spiritual enlightenment," meditation, and mindfulness. Back then, I was skeptical about such things. Bearing in mind I was only twenty-five years old at the time, I loved going out, clubbing, drinking, and meeting people. Meditation, mindfulness, and all that stuff seemed like something only monks or woo-woo spiritual people did.

Regardless, I decided to explore, and my journey with meditation began. After all, I had nothing to lose. It was free to do, and I could do it in my own time. So, in the middle of my bed for ten minutes a day, I sat cross-legged and practiced for ten days straight. After just one week, there was a noticeable change. My awareness was heightened. Food tasted better. I could hear, see, and think more clearly. In fact, everything was clearer. I even stopped drinking alcohol because it felt as though meditation had given me the same result. The overthinking was less. A light had come on.

Self-awareness

"Knowing yourself is the beginning of all wisdom." - Aristotle

One of the first steps to dealing with overthinking is to become aware of it. Realize that your mind is constantly active and creating thoughts. Stop what you're doing right now or the next time you're in bed, on a plane, or doing nothing, then just pay attention to your thoughts. Simply notice them as they pop up and pass by.

As Eckhart Tolle recounts in conversation with a student in his book, *The Power of Now*:

"Let me ask you this: can you be free of your mind whenever you want to? Have you found the 'off' button? You mean stop thinking altogether? No, I can't, except maybe for a moment or two. Then the mind is using you. You are unconsciously identified with it, so you don't even know that you are its slave."

Go ahead and enter your mind. Don't escape it. Almost everyone wants to run away from their mind and distract themselves with entertainment, partying, Netflix, and on and on. But the thoughts don't go away. When you're alone and it's just you and your mind, instead of running away, run into it. Tune into your mind. What's going on in there?

For most of us, it's narrating our experience as we see it.

"Oh, that's a cute cat..."

"What do I need to buy today...?"

"Is that guy checking me out?"

The process of verbalizing is an attempt to direct the experience of the world into the realm of your thoughts. Your verbalization becomes integrated with your other thoughts. This, in turn, contributes to your history and values. When there is a build-up of energy such as anxiety, fear, or desire, the voice becomes very noticeable. As the energy builds up inside, the voice talks because inside there is discomfort and the talking releases it. However, you will also notice that in states in which you're not really bothered by anything, it still talks. For example, you're walking in a shopping mall and it says things like, "Look at that woman! She's pretty!" or "I love that new dress; let's take a look."

When you watch all your thoughts, you will see that most of them don't make much sense. Understand that the thoughts you have don't define you. They are simply outputs of what your consciousness perceives.

And as Eckhart Tolle told me on that bus journey:

"The real you is the one inside that notices the voice talking. That is the way out. Become consciously aware of the voice. That awareness

is a doorway to the depths of your being."

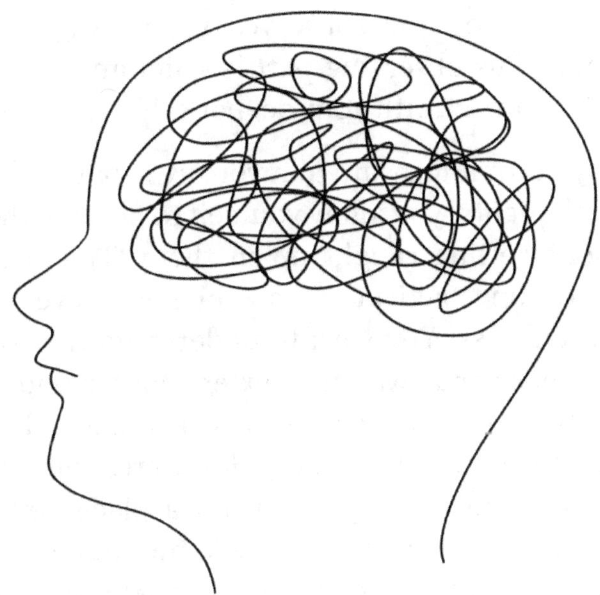

Mind identification

Becoming aware that you can notice and listen to your thoughts without getting caught up in them opens up a pathway to understanding a profound aspect of existence. Knowing about this observing part of yourself leads you to discover a significant truth about life and your place in it.

Identification with your thoughts is the barrier here. Mind identification can make you feel that you're under the control of these thoughts, as if they're an integral part of you. The key to gaining freedom from this state is to realize that you are not these thoughts; you are not the "thinker." The key to personal growth is recognizing that there is a part of you that observes your own mind's chatter. This observing part is quiet and offers a way to connect with your deeper self.

By becoming aware that you are separate from your thoughts, you allow yourself to observe them without getting caught up in them. This act of observation activates a higher level of consciousness. You start to understand that your intelligence and awareness extend far beyond just your thoughts. Moreover, this awareness helps you realize that true beauty, love, creativity, joy, and inner peace originate from a place beyond your mental processes. Acknowledging this distinction is what leads to a deeper awakening and understanding of yourself.

"There is nothing more important to true growth than realizing that you are not the voice of the mind, you are the one who hears it."

Ultimately, overthinking acts like a shield, helping you feel secure by trying to control your experiences and protect you from the world. However, this constant mental activity prevents you from fully engaging with life. Eventually, you will see that the real cause of problems is not life itself. It's the commotion the mind makes about life that causes problems. As you spend more time becoming self-aware, you will notice that the voice in your head never shuts up.

"Thoughts are going by like a river; awareness simply is." - Ram Dass

Have faith

As we conclude this chapter, we must acknowledge the role of faith in navigating the terrain of our minds and lives. Faith, as Eckhart Tolle suggests in *The Power of Now*, is the belief in something that cannot be proven with evidence and science. It is a reminder that the essence of our existence and the complexities of our consciousness extend beyond what can be quantified or analyzed.

For example, a group of scientists might present all the empirical evidence to argue that bananas are inherently bitter. However, one's direct experience can completely overturn this conclusion. The taste of a banana, sweet and unique, becomes a testament to the limitations of relying solely on intellectual arguments and empirical data. It underscores the importance of personal experience.

In this light, the journey through understanding and managing overthinking culminates in a call to faith. It is an invitation to trust in the unseen, to believe in the possibility of transformation and growth beyond what our current circumstances or past experiences might suggest. As we stand on the brink of new understandings and approaches to our mental processes, let us embrace faith not as a rejection of science but as a complementary force that propels us forward.

Therefore, as we turn the page, let it be with the faith that the steps we take into the unknown are guided not just by the knowledge we have accumulated but by the belief in the unseen currents that shape our lives. This faith, in ourselves and in the journey, is the first step toward transcending overthinking and embracing the fullness of our existence. Join me as we step out of the darkness and into the light.

CHALLENGE 4

Journaling is one of the best ways to gain more self-awareness, deal with overthinking, and gain clarity. By writing our thoughts down, we can break the cycle of negative thoughts and advance beyond where we may be trapped.

Writing a journal can be done on paper or on your phone notes. Even voice notes or video journals work well. Choose a time of the day to do this and stick with it. Try any of the following for a month.

How your day went

At the end of your day, write about how it went. Your minimum commitment is to write one good, one bad, and one thing you would change about the day. You can also make a list of three things you're grateful for, and then make a rough outline for the next day. This will keep you mentally light, make you more grateful, and give you purpose and things to look forward to. All it takes is just five to ten minutes.

____

____

____

____

Stream of thoughts

At the start of your day, write out your stream of thoughts. Just let them out onto the page. No censoring and no shame. The goal is simply to write stream-of-conscious journaling. This involves writing or speaking exactly what is going on in your head. Just let it all out. Aim to write one page. Again, it can take just five to ten minutes.

"Learn to work harder on yourself than you do on your job." - Jim Rohn

CHAPTER 4
FIND YOUR PURPOSE

Endless boredom, regret, and feeling tired all the time. You sleep six, seven, eight, nine, maybe ten hours or more. Sometimes you snooze, sometimes you sleep in. Yet you still feel tired. It's only 10 am and already you're surfing YouTube looking for some new videos. None look fun. So, you open up Instagram, Facebook, or TikTok. Whatever, you scroll for a bit. Hours later, you shamefully find yourself still stuck to the screen. You feel empty. The weekend is coming up and you have nothing to do. So, you get drunk on Saturday night and feel like trash all of Sunday. Soon enough it's Monday. Back to work, and you're already exhausted, facing a long week of boredom. The cycle repeats over and over again.

When we have days or hours on end that are empty, it is because our life lacks meaning. We lie in bed thinking what happened with my life? We fall into depression, have low motivation, waste time, and overthink. During the week, we get distracted by tasks, but a busy life often covers up deeper issues of fulfillment and purpose. When the weekend comes, especially Sunday, many have time to think and might start to notice a feeling of emptiness or a lack of meaning in their lives. "Sunday neurosis" refers to the feeling of sadness or emptiness some people experience on Sundays when they're not busy with work or their usual weekly activities. This realization can lead to a strong sense of unhappiness or depression. Unfortunately, for some people, this feeling can become so overwhelming that it contributes to thoughts of suicide.

The philosopher Schopenhauer mentioned that humans seemed to be stuck between feeling unhappy and being bored. Nowadays, boredom is becoming a bigger issue for mental health professionals than unhappiness. As technology advances and people have more free time, the problem might become even worse because many won't know how to use their extra time in a fulfilling way. Instead, many will fall into the traps of distraction, aversion, and compulsion.

When people feel a deep sense of emptiness and a lack of purpose in their lives, they often try to fill that void in various ways such as seeking power, money, and fame, as these can give a sense of success. Or by seeking pleasure, especially through sexual experiences, drugs, and alcohol. In the absence of a sense of purpose, the pursuit of pleasure can provide a temporary escape or a sense of fulfillment. However, these are just temporary solutions and don't address the underlying issue of finding a deeper meaning in life. Again, they are the traps of distraction, aversion, and compulsion.

"Results from a public opinion poll in France showed that over eighty percent of the people admitted they need 'something' to live for. Other sixty percent conceded that there was something, or someone, in their own lives for whose sake they were even ready to die."

Finding meaning

Viktor Frankl was an Austrian psychiatrist and a Holocaust survivor. During World War II, his experiences in Nazi concentration camps played a crucial role in shaping his theories. While in the camps, he observed that those who could find meaning in even the most horrendous of circumstances were more likely to survive. He noticed that fellow prisoners who had **a purpose, or something to look forward to**, showed greater resilience. He noticed that in the worst of conditions, in the darkest of times, those with the will or meaning to live were most likely to survive.

"He who has a reason to live can bear almost any how." - Nietzsche

Meaning or purpose is the reason we wake up in the morning feeling motivated. It could be something like your job. Or to be the best version of yourself. Or to be more mindful. Or to be a better leader. To write a book, to be a good partner, and so on. Purpose can change and adapt as life progresses.

Logotherapy

Frankl's own experiences of suffering, loss, and survival gave him a unique perspective on the importance of finding purpose in life. After his liberation from the concentration camps, he returned to Vienna where he continued his work as a psychiatrist and began to develop logotherapy as a formal theory. His seminal book, *Man's Search for Meaning*, outlines these ideas and his experiences in the concentration camps. To date, it remains one of the most influential works in psychotherapy and existential philosophy.

Logotherapy is based on the premise that our primary motivation in life is to find meaning rather than pursuing pleasure (as Freud suggested) or power (as Adler proposed).

Logotherapy aims to help individuals discover meaning in their lives, even under the most challenging circumstances, by leveraging the defiant power of the human spirit. Even in the most absurd, painful, or dehumanizing situations, life can have deep meaning.

According to Viktor Frankl, the search for meaning in life is not an introspective journey focused solely on one's inner world. Instead, it is an outward journey that involves engaging with the world around us. Logotherapy encourages patients to live as fully as possible. It proposes that the meaning of your life emerges from how you live it, particularly from the responsibility and intention you put into your actions. Our responsibility for our own lives is what imbues them with meaning. In embracing this responsibility, we don't just find the meaning of life; we actively create it through each action and decision. This shifts the focus from seeking an abstract, external meaning to recognizing that our meaning is crafted through our choices and actions.

Logotherapy emphasizes finding life's purpose through three main pathways.

- **Firstly**, it suggests that engaging in activities and creating things, whether through work, hobbies, or acts of kindness, can provide a sense of meaning. This encompasses everything from artistic expression to helping others and dedicating oneself to projects that are important to us.

- **Secondly**, logotherapy highlights the importance of our experiences and relationships. Meaning can be found in the moments we live and the connections we make with others. This includes profound experiences such as love, as well as simple pleasures such as enjoying nature.

- **Thirdly**, life will inevitably present us with challenges and suffering. In these moments, logotherapy encourages us to find meaning by choosing our attitude toward these difficulties. It's about discovering inner strength and resilience to overcome adversity and, possibly, growing from these experiences.

Paradoxical intention

One key part of logotherapy that plays an important role in overthinking is a technique called "paradoxical intention." Paradoxical intention encourages the individual to focus on what they fear. Fear is a powerful driving force for humans. For many of us, it is irrational or exaggerated. As such, it causes people to overthink and ultimately drives them away from what they want.

Paradoxical intention begins with identifying a specific fear or symptom that the patient is struggling with. For example, this might be insomnia, a fear of public speaking, or compulsive behavior. Instead of trying to avoid or suppress the fear, the patient is encouraged to do the opposite. They are instructed to wish or intend for the thing that they fear to happen. For instance, a person who is anxious about not being able to sleep might be told to go to bed and intentionally try to stay awake.

Often, this intentional engagement is done with a sense of exaggeration and humor. By willingly and exaggeratedly embracing the feared outcome, the patient is able to see the irrationality or absurdity of the fear, thus reducing its power. The paradox lies in the fact that by doing the opposite of what their anxiety is driving them to do, patients often find that their anxiety is reduced. When a person no longer resists the symptoms or fear, it loses its grip over them.

In the book *Man's search for meaning*, Viktor Frankl tells the story of a man who consulted him about his problem with excessively sweating:

"I advised the patient, in the event that sweating should recur, to resolve deliberately to show people how much he could sweat. He returned to report that whenever he met anyone who triggered his anxiety, he said to himself, 'I only sweated out a quart before, but now I'm going to pour at least ten quarts!' The result was that, after suffering from his phobia for four years, he was able to free himself permanently of it within one week."

As you can see, this technique helped to restore the patient's sense of control over his behavior. The effectiveness of paradoxical intention lies in its ability to break the cycle of anxiety and avoidance. By facing the fear head-on and even seeking it out, the patient learns that the feared outcome is not as threatening or unbearable as they thought. In conclusion, this can lead to a significant reduction in symptoms, a greater sense of control, and less overthinking.

Vision

"If you don't have a vision, if you don't have a goal and if you don't see your future laid out in front of you, you're just floating around without a purpose." - *Arnold Schwarzenegger*

Exploring the profound insights of logotherapy, Viktor Frankl's pioneering approach emphasizes the pursuit of meaning as the cornerstone of human motivation and healing. In summary, this therapeutic framework encourages individuals to transcend their current circumstances by living with meaning and envisioning a purposeful future. This notion aligns seamlessly with the concept of vision, which is vividly embodied by Arnold Schwarzenegger. The journey of a small-town boy from Austria to becoming one of the most recognizable figures in the world is a testament to the power of vision. It served as a beacon for him, illuminating a path from modest beginnings to extraordinary achievements. For someone entangled in overthinking, his story demonstrates how a clear vision can cut through the fog of indecision, providing direction and purpose.

"My first rule is to find your vision and follow it," Schwarzenegger advised. This guidance is especially pertinent for those prone to overthinking and negativity. The analogy of a ship navigating without a clear destination highlights the peril of aimless wandering. It's a scenario all too familiar to the overthinker, where the vast sea of possibilities leads to paralysis rather than choice. Schwarzenegger's wisdom suggests that defining a vision is akin to setting a course, a necessary first step to avoid drifting aimlessly in a sea of thoughts.

A well-defined vision gives one clarity and direction. It encourages moving from passive rumination to active pursuit of one's goals. In embracing this approach, we find a powerful strategy for transcending the limits of overthinking, inspired by Schwarzenegger's remarkable life journey. He dreamed of greatness in bodybuilding, acting, and public service. But he didn't just dream; he envisioned a future in which he achieved these goals. For someone caught in the cycle of negativity, the takeaway is clear: dreams become achievable not when we stop overthinking, but when we start directing our thoughts toward a defined vision.

Moreover, Schwarzenegger's journey highlights the importance of not thinking small. Overthinkers often limit themselves, bogged down by the details and potential pitfalls of each decision. However, by dreaming big and aiming for the stars, Schwarzenegger shows us the power of a vision that stretches beyond our immediate grasp. Such a vision compels us to move forward, to take risks, and to act despite our fears. It's a call to embrace the uncertainty that comes with pursuing a bold vision, using our capacity for deep thought not as a source of endless worry but as a springboard for ambitious goals.

In essence, Schwarzenegger's philosophy on vision offers a roadmap for navigating the complex terrain of overthinking. It encourages us to define our destination clearly, to dream big, and to channel our propensity for deep thought into the pursuit of our goals. Inspired by Schwarzenegger's example, we learn that the key to overcoming overthinking lies not in silencing our thoughts, but in aligning them with a clear and compelling vision of the future we wish to create.

"I was poor because I didn't have anything, but I was rich because I had a dream." - Arnold Schwarzenegger

The story of Arnold Schwarzenegger highlights how a clear vision can guide us from humble beginnings to remarkable achievements. This narrative complements Viktor Frankl's teachings on finding purpose and creating value in our lives, even amidst suffering.

In today's fast-paced world, full of distractions and the chase after fleeting pleasures, the search for meaning is now more important than ever. Frankl's work reminds us that purpose comes not from external achievements but through our response to life's challenges, our engagement with what truly matters, and the values we choose to live by. Meaning is crafted, not found. It's built through deliberate actions, relationships that matter, and choices that reflect who we are and aspire to be. Engaging with life courageously, embracing growth, and finding joy in the journey are key to cultivating a fulfilling existence.

Let Arnold's story and our exploration of logotherapy serve as a reminder that meaning is within reach, no matter where we start or what obstacles we face. Remember that overthinking can become your opportunity for growth. As Frankl suggests, it's not just about enduring life's trials but thriving because of them. Let's carry forward the lesson that our greatest potential lies in our ability to find purpose and joy in the journey, shaping ourselves and the world around us for the better.

CHALLENGE 5

Please pause for reflection here. Before reading further, answer the following questions. Or at the very least think about them for a few minutes. If you want more from this, then write them down and journal about them. Revisit them in the coming weeks, months, and years.

- *Where is your life going?*

____

____

____

____

- *What makes you feel alive?*

____

____

____

____

- *What energizes you?*

____

____

____

- *How do you want your days to look?*

____

____

____

____

- *What do you hate about your life?*

____

____

____

____

- *What are you going to do about it?*

- *What is your grand vision for your life? (Think on this for a long time.)*

Live Healthy
Drink Water
Eat Well
Relax More
Be Active

CHAPTER 5
BETTER LIVING

Imagine a charismatic young man dressed in a white, well-fitted, button-up shirt. He is in good shape, wearing black suit trousers and stylish, polished, black shoes. He smiles as he opens the door for an elderly gentleman. He compliments a waitress on her great service, even though she seems to be a little bit grumpy that day. As he walks down the street, he smiles at a stranger passing by. Visiting a local coffee shop, he chats with the owner, complimenting them on their new interior design. Everywhere he goes, he radiates positive energy.

Can you imagine such a person being depressed or worried, or overthinking? It's difficult to imagine. Such a lifestyle illustrates a profound truth: by extending our focus outward, we not only light up the paths of others but also illuminate our own. A pathway that is liberated from overthinking. Too much focus on ourselves causes us to get trapped in our thoughts and overthink. When you direct your focus outward onto others, it takes the pressure off you. The key is to get out of your head and into the world.

Our world is a huge place, and nowadays it's more connected than ever before. Please bear with me for a moment. I'm not going to get all woo-woo on you; neither will I try to convince you to rub a bowl or chant. However, it is my belief that all humans are connected at a higher level. Some call this God, the universe, or energy. Believing in this has served me well. One key way I've come to this realization is from traveling and experiencing different cultures. When you arrive in a new country, you can feel the culture and its vibe right away. Imagine how, when you visit large cities, the pace of life feels so fast. Imagine how peaceful a religious place feels. Think about how you often have a sixth sense about a person. Then it turns out to be true. Ultimately, we are atoms and stardust emanating from the Big Bang some 13.8 billion years ago. We all came from the same source, and thus we are all connected.

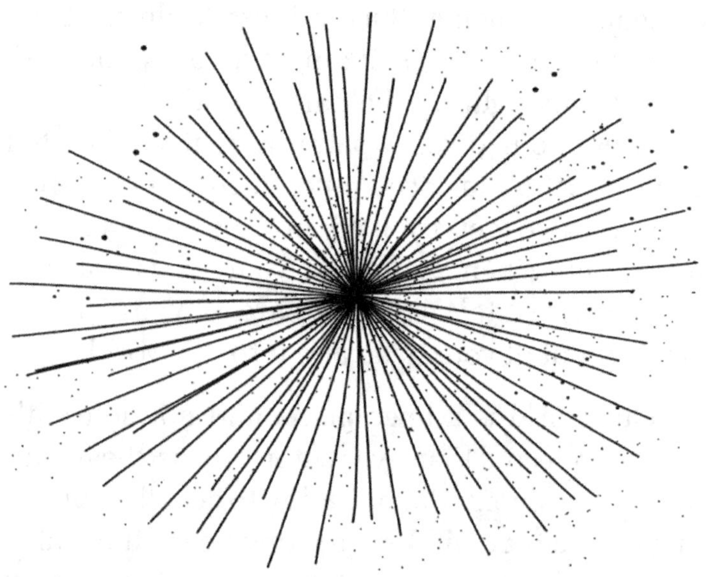

Think about when you feel moody and other

people annoy you. Or when you're out there smiling and good things happen. It's all part of that connection you have with the world. Do your best to connect positively with the other people in this world. I know some of you may be introverts or fear social interactions. Start small and mentally acknowledge other people. Think of something you like about them. Soon enough, your confidence will grow and your overthinking will shrink. As it grows, it compounds. You will soon feel comfortable saying hello or even smiling. Smiling is a gift to share. :) This will lead to conversations, which may lead to relationships. Along the way, you will face setbacks, negative reactions, and so on. The key is to not take it personally and to keep moving forward. It's really easy to start this. Surely you come across service staff? Ask them how they are. Be polite and friendly with them. Again, it all helps to take the attention off you.

As your social skills grow, start building a community. It will help to improve your mental health. Engaging in meaningful conversations and activities with friends and family helps a lot. Sharing our thoughts and feelings brings them out into the open. Moreover, the problems we face are not unique. Getting a fresh perspective on them might reveal a novel way to solve them. Ideally, talk with people who are solution-focused and good role models. Join your friends in activities that serve others. Again, it's all about taking the focus from inward to outward. By focusing on the world around you and how you can contribute to it, you will find a deeper, more meaningful life.

Healthy living

A bustling, purpose-driven life leaves little room for overthinking. Days filled with meaningful activities and routines leave less time to overthink. Set your life up in such a way that you have a good work-life balance. Don't just fill the down time with emptiness. Remember, we all need purpose and things to look forward to. Schedule a walk, a massage, or maybe just a drive, listening to music. There are countless hobbies and things to do each day, so don't waste your life on the couch. Action is the antidote. Furthermore, some problems that you're thinking about just need more time to pass by. Get busy in the meantime.

"When I can't handle events, I let them handle themselves." - Henry Ford

Stick to a daily routine. Wake up without any snooze button, hit the shower, brush your teeth, get dressed, and get to work. Make a to-do list for the day. Grab a pen and paper (or your phone, if you're digital like that) and jot down what you need to do. Make things tangible and actionable. Start ticking off those tasks on your list, one by one. Before you know it, you'll be making progress and feeling better about life.

Your health really is your wealth. Take care of your body and your mind will be healthier as a result. Establish a daily workout routine. Maybe it's lifting weights or some cardio. Better still, you could join an exercise class. Samuel Untermyer, a prominent American lawyer, had a unique approach to overthinking and exercise. He noted that during a period of intense depression, he pushed himself to be physically active almost every hour. His mornings were filled with several sets of tennis, followed by a bath, lunch, and then eighteen holes of golf in the afternoon. On Friday nights, he would dance until one in the morning.

"I am a firm believer in the power of sweating out depression and worry." - Samuel Untermyer

Sleep

Studies and research have shown that sleep plays a crucial role in maintaining and improving our health. According to the National Institutes of Health (NIH), sleep is not merely downtime for the brain but a critical period for brain work, including learning, memory formation, and toxin removal. Lack of sleep is a common problem for overthinkers. They lie in bed at night unable to switch off their minds and sleep. As a result, the next day they are tired and grumpy. Some may resort to sleeping pills or drugs to switch off. But reliance on drugs eventually builds tolerance and it can spiral out of control.

Instead of doing that, choose some natural ways to get better sleep. First of all, aim to stick to a fixed wake-up time and bedtime. Typically, people with mental health issues are random with their sleep times. By setting a fixed sleep and wake-up time, your body adjusts to the routine, which allows it adequate recovery time. Now I know it's easy to say just get in bed at 11 pm. But what if my mind won't switch off? Give it time. Set your alarm and bedtime. Eventually, your body will adjust.

Moreover, to help you switch off, you need a wind-down routine. Ideally, you should be away from any devices for at least an hour before bed. Choose low-stimulation activities such as reading biographies. I try to use a second phone in my bedroom that is only for reading books and alarms. It does nothing else. I also have a dim light setting on it for reading. You can try a Kindle or hardcopy books as well. Do some journaling before bed and/or a short meditation. Aim to clear everything from your mind.

Now if you still struggle with sleep, then maybe watch a movie or a series. Find what works for you. Sex is good too because we sleep better after it. Spend those quality moments with your partner. Often an extra hour of sex will give you a deeper sleep. Or you can try the Samuel Untermyer approach to overthinking and exercise. Get up and either work or read until you feel sleepy.

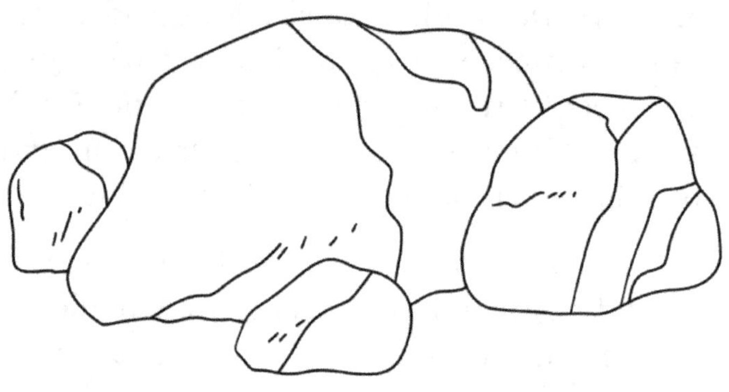

Antifragile

Even though we may build a healthy lifestyle, it can still be threatened by the uncertainty of living in a world that's unpredictable and full of challenges. But we should not seek to just survive but thrive amidst the chaos. The key to such a thriving existence might be found in an innovative concept called antifragility, introduced by the author Nassim Nicholas Taleb.

Building an antifragile life begins with defining what you don't want in your life. Maybe you don't want excess body fat, or you don't want to be poor or lonely. What brings you negativity or causes you to overthink? Having awareness of those issues will help you to eliminate them. From there, you can build a safety net in the form of backups (financial, emotional, or physical) to lay a foundation of stability. Have an emergency fund, keep a spare tire in your vehicle, establish multiple incomes, develop your social circles, and backup your work. This preparedness will not only shield you but will make your life more stable, and you'll be stronger as a result.

Next is to work on how you deal with stress. It's going to show up, especially for those who strive to become better. Have the mentality of bringing it on. Be brave enough to face problems head-on because by doing so, you can build mental toughness. Practice it in small ways such as taking cold showers, eating a simple diet, and so on.

As we navigate through life's inevitable stresses, adopting an antifragile mindset empowers us. Facing challenges head-on, whether through cultivating mental toughness in the face of adversity or finding solace in the discomfort of a cold shower, prepares us for the complexities of life. It's in these moments of discomfort that we find our strength, forging an existence where overthinking loses its grip on our minds. Become comfortable with the uncomfortable and you'll find strength from it.

Building a healthy lifestyle is a pathway to success, and it is an ongoing journey. A journey of learning and stacking up the wins. Keep on building positive momentum. Those small wins will accumulate. Even small things, such as overcoming the inertia to go to the gym or talking to strangers. Do more of what you love and work hard. If you make a mistake, learn from it. All of us make mistakes. You can't change what happened, but you can learn from it. That's the key. Improving your lifestyle will take some effort. But the return is worth it.

CHALLENGE 6

Start building a healthy lifestyle. Find at least three events or group meetups in your area for you to attend this month. Facebook, Meetup, and Google are great ways to find such things. Find them and go to them. You got this.

CHAPTER 6
THE POWER OF NOW

Once upon a time, in the bustling city of Nowhere, lived a young woman named Rina. Her life was a whirlwind of events, deadlines, and constant digital notifications. Each day blended into the next, a blur of tasks and responsibilities. Amid this chaos, she stumbled upon a concept that seemed almost magical in its simplicity and promise: mindfulness.

Mindfulness, as Rina learned, was the art of being fully present in the moment. Paying attention to the here and now, without judgment or distraction. Intrigued by the idea, she decided to embark on a journey to integrate mindfulness into her life. Her first encounter with mindfulness was on a busy morning, amidst the chaos of city life. Instead of rushing through breakfast, she sat quietly, taking the time to savor each bite. She noticed the texture of the bread, the sweetness of the jam, and the richness of the coffee. It was a simple act, yet for the first time in a long while, she felt a sense of calm and appreciation for the moment.

Encouraged by this experience, Rina began to explore mindfulness in other aspects of her life. Walking to work, instead of being lost in thought or glued to a smartphone screen, she noticed the feel of the sun on her skin. The vibrant colors of the trees and the sounds of the city. Each step became a meditation, walking in the present. At work, instead of succumbing to the overwhelming rush of tasks, Rina practiced mindful breathing during breaks. Focusing on her breath, inhaling deeply and exhaling slowly. In such moments, she found an island of peace amidst the sea of stress. It helped her approach tasks with a clearer mind and more focused attention.

Mindfulness also transformed Rina's interactions with others. In conversations, she learned to listen actively. She gave her full attention to the speaker, without planning a response or being judgmental. Such openness fostered deeper connections and understanding. Mundane exchanges transformed into meaningful conversations.

Yet, the journey was not without its challenges. There were days when her mind wandered incessantly. Moments of frustration and impatience crept in. But with each stumble, she returned to her breathing and the present moment. It was all a gentle reminder to be kind and patient. As days turned into weeks, and weeks into months, the practice of mindfulness began to weave a profound change in Rina's life. The constant noise of her mind began to quieten, replaced by a sense of peace and contentment. Life's challenges remained, but she faced them with a new resilience, grounded in the present moment.

"Life unfolds in the present." - Eckhart Tolle

Become the witness of your life

Life is happening here and now, at this moment. The past is nothing more than present moments that have passed us by. The future is a collection of present moments that will happen. Overthinking is what distracts us from the present, as our thoughts carry us away on a never-ending stream. But we can choose whether to jump into the thoughts, swim through them, or watch them from the sides.

Mindfulness will connect you with what is going on here and now. It is the simplest yet most powerful concept of life, and it is available to you at any time. From the simplest of activities to the most thrilling, you can choose to be mindful at any moment. Life will be experienced fully when you detach from your thoughts and are present in the moment.

"Those who have not found their true wealth, which is the radiant joy of being, are beggars, even if they have great material wealth. They are looking outside for scraps of pleasure or fulfillment, while they have a treasure within that not only includes all those things but is infinitely greater than anything the world can offer."

Overthinking is the barrier to mindfulness. Everything you need to be mindful is already within you. It begins with paying attention to what's going on here and now. It's not about thinking; rather, it is about paying attention. You don't need to study, over-analyze, and overthink everything. You can simply be in the moment and bring awareness to your life. There is no judgment, no dialogue. It's just being the witness of your life.

Some say life is predetermined, that we cannot change our fate because our biology determines our pathway. Our existence can be traced back to the Big Bang. We are essentially star dust, particles and atoms moving on from that explosion. Moving on without being able to do anything to change our fate. There is much scientific evidence to prove this. If it is true, then we must be more present to witness the beauty of its unfolding. Be aware of your thoughts or the feeling of eating or walking. Whatever it is you're doing, be present in it. Mindfulness will grow with consistency and practice, just as a seed grows with water or a muscle grows with repetition. Mindfulness will bring you more inner peace.

"Mindfulness is awareness that arises through paying attention, on purpose, in the present moment, non-judgmentally." - Jon Kabat-Zinn, creator of the program Mindfulness-Based Stress Reduction (MBSR)

Distraction

A study conducted by the University of San Diego discovered that when we're distracted, it triggers a flight-or-flight response. Every time you receive notifications or something that takes you away from what you're currently doing, it derails your focus. In the grand scheme of life, such small distractions can take you away from a bigger purpose.

Multitasking is counterproductive, and it's one of the biggest inhibitors of mindfulness. Even when we're doing the simple things, we should do them completely and fully. Do one thing at a time and be mindful when you're doing it. As the parable says, a rabbit trying to go down two holes goes down none. If you want to think constructively, for example, about an important decision, then be still and only think of that one thing. If you're going to do the dishes, do only the dishes. Don't distract yourself with music or podcasts. Make a conscious effort to create a calm environment. Remove things that distract you or take away your focus. Do one thing at a time and stop multitasking.

- Close all the browser tabs except for the one you're working on.
- Remove any apps on your phone that distract you.
- Put your phone on silent and get some stuff done. You can always look at them later.

The key is to do one thing at a time.

Practice it for a while and see how it brings you

calmness. At the gym, give your full attention to the workout. Focus your mind on lifting the weights. Don't get carried away by drifting thoughts. Be completely in the moment. As you read these words, take them all in with your full presence. Breathe in the experience of life and immerse yourself in it. Every time you touch, smell, and taste, take the moment to enjoy it fully there and then. In doing so, you will find that there's so much joy to be had, even in the simplest of precious things.

"An ordered mind is a happy mind, and when we can't make sense of our place in this world by understanding our connection to it, our actions lose meaning." - Dan Koe

Meditation

Meditation will help you to cultivate more mindfulness in your life. Truly, it is one of the most undervalued skills. I believe that if every person in the world practiced it, we would have far fewer problems.

Over five thousand years ago, the seeds of meditation were sown within the cradle of civilization now known as India. The ancient Vedas, scriptures sacred to Hinduism, first documented meditation techniques as a means to transcend physical existence and unite with the divine. This practice was not merely spiritual. It was a way of life, intertwining with daily routines to foster a deep connection to the cosmos and the inner self.

As centuries turned, meditation voyaged eastward with the spread of Buddhism. Siddhartha Gautama, the Buddha, in the 6th century BCE, after a profound experience of enlightenment under the Bodhi tree, propagated meditation as a core element of his teachings. It was through meditation that one could extinguish the flames of desire and suffering, achieving Nirvana, the ultimate state of liberation and peace. Buddhism's expansion across Asia carried these practices to the heartlands of China, Korea, Japan, and beyond, each culture infusing it with its own essence, giving rise to diverse traditions such as Zen and Vipassana.

Today, meditation is a global phenomenon that has adapted to the needs of modern life, offering solace in the face of the relentless pace of the 21st century. From mindfulness-based stress reduction programs to corporate wellness initiatives, meditation has proven its versatility and relevance, a testament to its enduring legacy.

The science of meditation

In 2005, Sara Lazar, a Harvard neuroscientist, published some interesting discoveries from her research on meditation. She discovered that meditation could change the brain structure. In her studies, it was found that meditators developed a thicker cortex. That is the part of the brain that is responsible for controlling attention and emotion. Amazingly, their brains had developed a stronger attention span in as little as eight weeks of daily meditation practice.

In addition, neuroimaging technologies, such as functional magnetic resonance imaging (fMRI) and electroencephalography (EEG), have revealed that meditation can lead to significant changes in brain structure and function. Studies have shown increases in gray matter density in areas of the brain associated with memory, learning, and empathy, such as the hippocampus and areas of the prefrontal cortex. Conversely, regions involved in stress and anxiety, such as the amygdala, show decreased activity in meditators.

Psychologically, meditation has been linked to enhanced emotional well-being and reduced symptoms of mental health conditions such as depression, anxiety, and PTSD. The practice is believed to improve emotional regulation by fostering a non-judgmental awareness of the present moment, allowing individuals to experience thoughts and feelings without being overwhelmed by them. This mindfulness aspect of meditation helps break the negative cycles of overthinking.

Meditation's ability to reduce stress is perhaps one of its most celebrated benefits. Through practices such as mindfulness meditation, individuals can learn to diminish the physiological responses to stress, lowering cortisol levels and reducing the overall impact of stress on the body. This reduced stress response has also been linked to improved immune function, with some studies suggesting that regular meditation can enhance the body's ability to fight off illness.

Beyond mental health and stress reduction, meditation has been studied for its potential physical health benefits. Research indicates that it can contribute to lower blood pressure, reduced chronic pain, and improved sleep patterns. These effects are thought to be mediated through the relaxation response, a physiological state of deep rest that changes the physical and emotional responses to stress.

Meditation practices

Meditation encompasses a diverse array of practices across various cultures and traditions, each with its unique approach and objectives. Here's a very brief overview of some of the major schools or practices of meditation:

- **Mindfulness Meditation**: Originating from Buddhist teachings, this practice involves paying attention to thoughts, feelings, and sensations in the present moment without judgment.
- **Transcendental Meditation** (TM): A form of silent mantra meditation developed by Maharishi Mahesh Yogi. Practitioners use a specific mantra given to them by a trained teacher to transcend ordinary thought and reach a state of pure consciousness.
- **Zen Meditation** (Zazen): Rooted in Buddhist tradition, Zazen involves sitting in precise postures and focusing on the breath, sometimes with concentration on a koan (a paradoxical

anecdote or riddle) to train the mind and realize the nature of existence.

- **Vipassana Meditation**: One of the oldest forms of meditation in India, Vipassana means "to see things as they really are." It involves practicing self-observation by focusing on the interconnection between the mind and body through the breath and physical sensations.

- **Loving-Kindness Meditation (Metta)**: This practice is aimed at developing unconditional, inclusive love and kindness toward oneself and others. It involves repeating phrases of goodwill and compassion toward oneself and others, gradually expanding the circle of care.

- **Yoga Meditation**: Encompasses a variety of practices from the yogic tradition, including breath control (pranayama), the use of postures (asanas), and meditation on a divine aspect or mantra (dhyana). It aims to achieve spiritual growth and physical health.

- **Religious Meditation**: Involves contemplation and prayer to deepen one's relationship with God. It depends on religious belief. Christian, Muslim, Jewish, and all other religions have a form of prayer.
- **Sufi Meditation**: Includes practices such as dhikr (remembrance of God), in which practitioners repeat divine names or phrases to draw closer to the divine presence.
- **Taoist Meditation**: Focuses on harmony with the Tao, or the fundamental nature of the universe. Practices include concentration, visualization, and breathing techniques to cultivate energy flow and spiritual insight.
- **Qigong and Tai Chi**: These are traditional Chinese practices that combine meditation, breathing techniques, and movement to enhance the flow of qi (vital energy) throughout the body, promoting health and spiritual well-being.

Each of these schools or practices of meditation offers a unique path to personal growth, well-being, and spiritual insight, reflecting the rich tapestry of human culture and spirituality. I know it's overwhelming and confusing. Navigating the diverse landscape of meditation practices can feel like standing at the crossroads of a vast and ancient map, each path offering its unique journey inward.

- Personally, I have found the simplest and most effective to be Vipassana and Mindfulness. Using apps is more of a step outside of your mind, and I wouldn't recommend them. Perhaps they are helpful for getting started but not for the long term.

How to meditate

Choose the meditation style that resonates with you. If the serene focus of Zen meditation calls to you, or if the heartfelt warmth of Metta stirs something deep within, let your intuition guide you. There's no "right" choice, only the right choice for you. Remember, the goal isn't perfection; it's presence.

Here is a simple meditation you can do.

- Step one: Choose a quiet place and position that is comfortable but not too comfortable. Slouching or lying down is too much comfort. Rigid posture is too uncomfortable. Strive for a balance between comfort and alertness in which you can sit alert for a long time. Sitting on a chair or cross-legged on a cushion is good.

- Step two: Set a timer. You can do this on your phone but turn the data off, so you won't get notifications or distractions. Set the time for five minutes. As you become more comfortable with it, you can gradually go for twenty minutes, which is the sweet spot of daily practice.

- Step three: Close your eyes. Become aware of your body. Breathe deeply in. Notice how the air comes through the tip of your nose as you inhale. Notice how it fills up your lungs and how your diaphragm expands. Focus completely on your breathing. Let go of all thoughts. If they come up in your mind, forgive yourself. Just watch them pass like leaves in the wind. Don't get attached to them. If you do, forgive yourself and come back to the present moment.

- Step four: When the timer goes off, slowly

open your eyes. Smile. Stretch your body and notice your environment. Give thanks for this moment.

Walking meditation is another simple practice you can do. Just find a place with space for you to walk. Even better if it's barefoot so you can feel the textures underneath your feet. Walk slowly and with intent. As you take each step, focus on the sensation of rising and falling.

Yes, meditation really is that simple. The results come the more you practice it. You'll soon notice how much more connected you feel with life. Food will taste better, thinking will be clearer, and life will have more clarity. Eventually, that will become your new normal. Stick with it.

Make meditation a habit in your life. Consistency is key. Try to meditate at the same time each day. Maybe in the morning, as a serene start to your day, or in the evening, as a quieting end. This regularity builds a habit, weaving meditation into the fabric of your daily life.

Be patient with yourself. Meditation is a journey inward, and like all journeys, it involves both smooth passages and rough terrain. Some days, your mind may be a whirlwind of thoughts. On others, a pool of stillness. Each experience is part of the process, teaching you about yourself.

Approach your practice with compassion, celebrating your efforts and intentions to engage in this transformative work.

Remember, you're not alone. Many before you have walked this path and many more will follow. Connecting with a community, whether online, through a meditation center, or with friends who also meditate can offer support.

Dopamine detox

One last suggestion I have is to try a meditation retreat. Many call it a digital detox. These can last anywhere from one to thirty days. It involves going to an isolated place such as a temple or facility with accommodation and space for meditation. Once there, you will follow a full schedule of daily meditations with other people. You eat, sleep, and meditate there. The schedule includes fixed times for each activity.

Often these retreats are in silence. As a result, I often notice the energies of people on a deeper level. Bear with me for a moment as I explain. As a result of the silence, you pay more attention to body language and the presence of people. As I'm sure you're aware, many studies show that we communicate mostly non-verbally. A silent retreat keenly tunes you into this.

Overall, what you'll gain from a retreat is that it brings you intensely into the present moment. Truly, you are confronted with all your inner dialogue, and that breaks down the ego. In the process, you will gain clarity and intent in your life. I try to do one once a year and always get a ton of value from it.

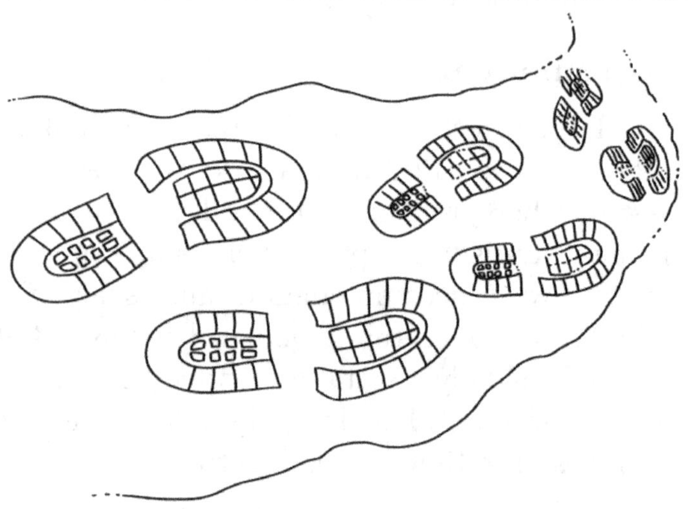

As we conclude our journey exploring mindfulness, we appreciate its essence, that is, the art of being present in each moment, free from judgment and distraction. Mindfulness teaches us to relish life's nuances, from the taste of our meals to the warmth of sunlight or a friend's voice. These practices not only deepen our appreciation of the present moment but also foster a sense of calm and freedom from overthinking.

Integrating mindfulness into our daily lives enhances focus and clarity, transforming work and creativity by fostering a calm, centered approach to tasks. It enriches relationships too, through active listening and genuine engagement, turning routine interactions into meaningful connections.

The path to mindfulness, however, is not without challenges. Distractions and frustrations test our commitment, reminding us to return to the present with kindness and patience. Yet, with practice, mindfulness becomes a part of us, quieting mental noise and instilling peace and resilience.

Ultimately, mindfulness is more than a personal journey; it's a way to live more deeply, fostering inner peace and contributing positively to those around us. Each moment offers a new opportunity to engage with life's beauty, leading to a more intentional and aware existence.

CHALLENGE 7

Meditation. Try it for ten days consecutively and aim for ten minutes a day. Choose any of the methods outlined in the previous chapter, or follow the guided meditation in that chapter, repeated here. Notice how you feel after 10 consecutive days.

- **Step one:** Choose a quiet place and position that is comfortable but not too comfortable. Slouching or lying down is too much comfort. Rigid posture is too uncomfortable. Strive for a balance between comfort and alertness in which you can sit alert for a long time. Sitting on a chair or cross-legged on a cushion is good.
- **Step two:** Set a timer. You can do this on your phone, but turn the data off so you won't get notifications or distractions. Set the time for five minutes. As you become more comfortable with it, you can gradually go for twenty minutes, which is the sweet spot of daily practice.
- **Step three**: Close your eyes. Become aware of your body. Breathe deeply in. Notice how the air comes through the tip of your nose as you inhale. Notice how it fills up your lungs and how your diaphragm

expands. Focus completely on your breathing. Let go of all thoughts. If they come up in your mind, forgive yourself. Just watch them pass like leaves in the wind. Don't get attached to them. If you do, forgive yourself and come back to the present moment.

- **Step four**: When the timer goes off, slowly open your eyes. Smile. Stretch your body and notice your environment. Give thanks for this moment.

Make meditation a habit in your life. Consistency is key. Try to meditate at the same time each day. Maybe in the morning, as a serene start to your day, or in the evening, as a quieting end.

____

____

____

____

____

CHAPTER 7
HOW TO MAKE DECISIONS

I recently found myself on the quest to buy a new motorcycle. My goal was to find one suitable for inner-city commuting. To give you some background, I live in the center of Bangkok, Thailand. It is one of the most congested cities on the planet. People tend to navigate this maze on scooters, dodging and zipping between the traffic jams with ease. After a recent thrilling ride on a big 500cc motorcycle, I was hooked on the adrenaline. That ride was nothing short of electrifying and it had me daydreaming about bringing that buzz into the city streets.

The big kid in me wanted it, but cruising through Bangkok on a beast like that was more fantasy than practicality. Imagine it—no space to store anything, the engine's heat turning your commute into a sauna, all while you're stuck in the same gridlock you'd face in a car. The logical choice? A nimble scooter tailor-made for the congested traffic. Yet, the heart wants what it wants, and mine was set on that big bike. I went so far as to pick one out and start the paperwork for registration. But then, the reality check: second thoughts began to cloud my excitement. Was I letting my emotions steer me? It took a few rounds of mental tug-of-war before I called off the deal, realizing I had let my excitement get the better of my judgment. In the process, I unfortunately wasted the seller's time and my own.

Through this experience, I learned the importance of balancing emotion with practicality, ensuring that my decisions truly align with reality. As you will discover in this chapter, sometimes, the rush of a momentary thrill can cloud our judgment, leading us down paths that don't quite fit our reality.

"It is in your moments of decision that your destiny is shaped." - Tony Robbins

If you go into a supermarket these days, you're going to be presented with multiple choices: six different types of milk, ten different types of bread, and that's just the food! Every day, people are bombarded with multiple career paths to choose between, endless holiday destinations, and infinite lifestyle options. There's never been more choice than now, which is great, but it also makes it difficult for us to think clearly and decide.

Buridan's Ass

A donkey is facing a dilemma of choice as described by the French philosopher Jean Buridan. The donkey sits between two haystacks that are equal in distance, size, and composition. As it looks from one to the other, it finds itself trapped in an impossible conundrum. Which one should I choose? Minutes, hours, and days pass by as the donkey stands there undecided, until one day, it suffers the tragic consequences of indecision and dies of starvation.

Understand that not making a timely decision is also a decision that will often leave you in a worse situation. That can be aggravated by the availability of too many options. This is the problem with indecision, often referred to as analysis paralysis. It leads to overthinking, which all results in your feeling overwhelmed and unable to decide.

The Pope asked Michelangelo: "How have you created the statue of David, the masterpiece of all masterpieces?" Michelangelo's answer: "It's simple. I removed everything that is not David."

Trying to make decisions where we are gathering lots of information and considering different viewpoints can cause us to overthink. When we seek too many opinions and options, it often makes decision-making even harder. Some of this is fine, but you need to draw the line somewhere. I'm sure you've been there. Writing down pros and cons. Analyzing which is a better option. But in most cases, the differences are so small that it doesn't really matter. Does any of the following sound familiar?

- You constantly seek more information without reaching any conclusion.
- You fear making the wrong decision, which causes you to put it off.
- You worry excessively and can't gain clarity.
- You miss deadlines due to struggling to make a choice.
- You feel stressed, anxious, and/or overwhelmed.
- You constantly feel tired and burned out.

- You constantly seek the opinions of others, even when you have more than enough input.

Certain ways of thinking can make this worse:

- **Rigid thinking**: Seeing things in black and white can make complex decisions feel overwhelming because they don't fit neatly into a particular category.
- **Perfectionism**: Wanting to make the perfect choice can freeze us in our tracks, especially when decisions have big impacts on our lives or others'.
- **People pleasing**: Trying to make everyone happy can make us afraid to make any decision at all.
- **Lack of confidence**: Not trusting ourselves to make good choices can lead us to endlessly seek advice and second-guess ourselves.
- **Empathy**: Worrying about how our decisions will affect others can make us hesitant to decide anything.

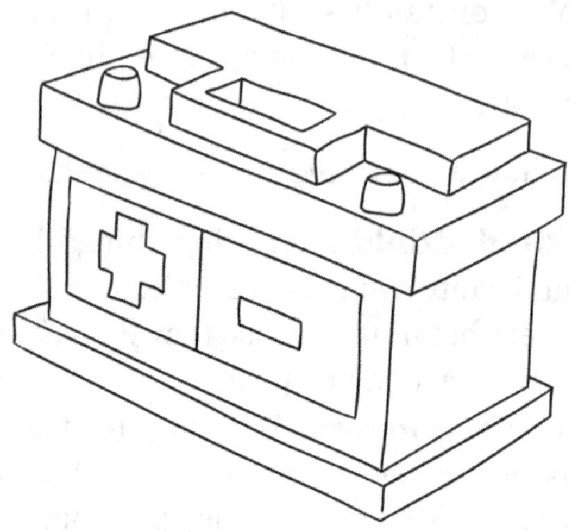

Choice is a finite resource

Imagine your brain as a battery that starts each day fully charged. Every decision, from the trivial to the significant, draws a little power from this battery. As the day progresses and you continue to make decisions, the battery drains. This depletion of mental energy leads to decision fatigue. At the heart of decision fatigue is the understanding that our ability to weigh choices is a finite resource. When we use up this resource, our decision-making skills deteriorate.

It's not just the big, life-changing decisions that wear us down; small, everyday choices such as what to eat for breakfast or which shirt to wear also chip away at our mental reserves. This is why, by the end of a long day of constant decision-making, a person might find themselves mindlessly scrolling through TV channels, unable to decide what to watch, or making impulsive, bad decisions.

What makes decision fatigue particularly insidious is that it's not always conscious. You might not feel tired in a traditional sense, but your brain's capacity to make thoughtful, well-considered choices diminishes. This can lead to two main outcomes. Either you become reckless, making impulsive decisions without fully considering the consequences, or you might do the exact opposite, avoiding decisions altogether. In a state of decision fatigue, the path of least resistance becomes the most appealing, whether that means making a hasty choice or none at all.

Firstly, to combat decision fatigue, it's essential to recognize that not all decisions are created equal. Prioritizing decisions and simplifying the number of choices we face daily can help preserve our decision-making energy. Some of the world's most successful people reduce decision fatigue by eliminating trivial choices. For example, wearing a similar outfit every day or eating the same breakfast each morning can conserve mental energy for more critical decisions.

Here are some practical tips:

- **Simplify your wardrobe**: Like Steve Jobs with his iconic black turtleneck, simplifying your wardrobe reduces the number of choices you have to make about what to wear each day. Choosing a sort of personal uniform or having a set rotation of outfits can save you time and mental energy.
- **Develop daily routines**: Establishing daily routines for regular activities (such as morning rituals, workout schedules, or evening relaxation practices) removes the need to decide on these activities daily. When actions become habitual, they require much less mental effort.
- **Plan meals in advance**: Decide on your meals for the week ahead and prepare them in batches if possible. This reduces daily decisions about what to eat and minimizes the effort of last-minute grocery shopping or cooking.
- **Limit choices**: Whether it's for shopping, entertainment, or work tasks, limit the options you have to choose from. Too many choices can be overwhelming and draining. Applying constraints can make decisions quicker and less taxing.
- **Delegate decisions**: If possible, delegate less important decisions to others. This

could mean letting a family member choose the movie for the night or having team members make small project decisions at work.

- **Use technology wisely**: Automate decisions where possible. Use apps and tools for tasks such as budgeting, scheduling, and reminders. Automation can take care of repetitive decisions, freeing up your mental space.

- **Prioritize your decisions**: Not all decisions deserve the same amount of your attention. Focus your energy on big, important decisions. For less critical choices, go with your first reasonable option rather than weighing every possibility. I'll discuss this in more detail soon.

- **Create if-then rules:** Develop personal policies or if-then rules for common decisions. For example, "If it's a workday, then I'll have a smoothie for breakfast" or "If a purchase is over $100, then I'll think it over for 24 hours before buying."

- **Practice mindfulness and stress reduction**: Mindfulness practices such as meditation can increase your mental clarity and resilience, making it easier to make decisions without feeling overwhelmed.

- **Set decision-making times**: Allocate specific times for making decisions. For instance, set aside time in the morning to plan your day or make significant work-related decisions. Knowing you have a designated time to make these decisions can reduce anxiety and improve focus.

By understanding these dynamics and adjusting your approach, you can navigate decisions more smoothly and with less stress. Your mental bandwidth will be free for the big stuff. Moving on, let's dive into how to make those important decisions.

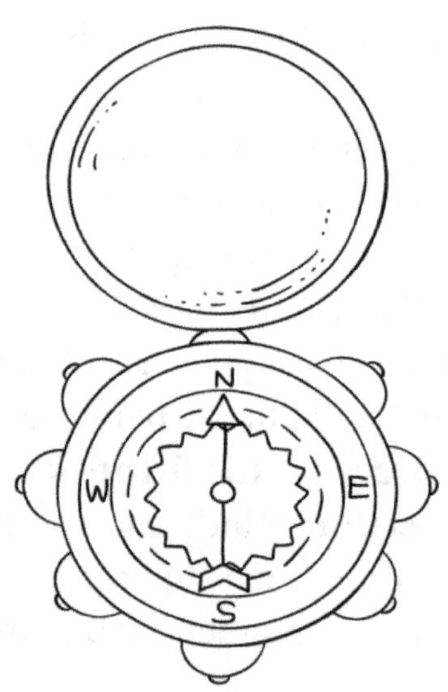

The decision-making process

As you already know, we make thousands of decisions daily and most are on autopilot. In his book *Thinking Fast and Slow*, Daniel Kahneman explains that we have two systems of thinking.

- **System one thinking** - This is our initial, autopilot response. Whilst this is time productive, it can also go against our interests. Sometimes we might have unhelpful, automatic overreactions, for example, overthinking social interactions that might cause us to avoid people.
- **System two thinking** - This is our conscious thinking. It helps us to focus our attention and exert self-control. It is the key difference which sets us apart from animals.

Fundamentally, our brain is lazy and has created shortcuts for the multitude of things that we encounter each day. In many cases, system one and system two don't work so well together. System one often tries to take over and may cause us to make a mistake. In doing so, it thinks it will save us energy.

When system one is incapable of handling the task at hand, system two takes over. However, you must be aware of the fallibility of these systems and understand when your emotions are confusing you, especially with logical things such as money. All too often, people make hasty, emotional decisions that might seem good now but will hurt them later.

"Don't let emotions get in the way where they have no business. After all, rule number 1 for any good poker player is 'Leave your emotions at home.'"

Each time you make important decisions, those that are beyond system one, you should follow a system. In these decisions, you will need to think carefully. Not overthink but think constructively.

Big decisions

When it comes to making big decisions in life, it's important to set aside a reasonable amount of time to think constructively and follow a system. First make an assessment of the decision's magnitude. Categorize it as either significant or minor.

- **For significant decisions**: A rational, checklist-based approach is used to methodically evaluate options and avoid common errors.

- **For minor decisions**: Intuition guides the decision-making process, allowing for quick, effortless choices.

Imagine you're trying to decide what to have for dinner. Rational optimization is like sitting down and thinking through your options very carefully. You consider everything from how hungry you are to what ingredients you have, how much time and effort you want to spend cooking, and even how healthy you want the meal to be.

It's like making a list of all your dinner options, then going through that list to pick the one that checks the most boxes for what's important to you at that moment. So, if you're super hungry, short on time, and have eggs in the fridge, you might decide that making an omelet is the best choice. In other words, it's about making decisions in an organized way, aiming to get the best possible outcome based on what matters most to you.

In everyday language, rational optimization is just a fancy way of saying "think through your choices and pick the best one for your situation." It's about taking a moment to consider your needs, what you have available, and what you're trying to achieve, then making the best decision based on those factors.

Now let's explore a scenario. Choosing what

city to live in is a big decision that perfectly suits a rational optimization approach. Let's break it down into simple, relatable steps:

Step one, collect the facts

In order to make better decisions, we have to concentrate our mind on the problem. Begin by collecting the facts but try to keep your emotions out of it. Collect the facts in an impartial, objective manner. An effective method is to imagine you're collecting the facts not for yourself but for someone else. This will put you in the frame of collecting evidence and, by doing so, remove the emotion.

Collect as much information as necessary. Consult with others for diverse viewpoints and do your research. Like when I was choosing a motorcycle. The real turning point came with some grounded advice from friends well-versed in navigating life's decision-making roads. They reminded me that getting swept away by the thrill of the moment can lead us astray. Be very diligent with this, but don't overdo it. Have a cut-off time.

"Neither you nor I nor Einstein nor the Supreme Court of the United States is brilliant enough to reach an intelligent decision on any problem without first getting the facts."

Step two, think about it

Susan Kay Nolen-Hoeksema, an American professor of psychology at Yale University, recommended scheduling a dedicated time to think about any important decisions you're facing. In his book *The Magic of Thinking Big*, D.J. Schwartz also suggests setting aside time to think.

"I insist on spending a lot of time thinking, almost every day, to just sit and think. That is very uncommon in American business. I read and think. So, I do more reading and thinking, and make less impulse decisions than most people in business. I do it because I like this kind of life." - Warren Buffett

Keith Cunnigham, in his excellent book *The Road Less Stupid*, suggests at least three thinking sessions a week. Turn off your phone for forty-five minutes to one hour. Sit still in a chair with a pen and paper nearby.

In your thinking session, get specific. Ask yourself:

1. *What do I want to do?*

2. *What are my options?*

3. *What are the factors?*

4. *What can I do about it?*

Write down anything important. Keep adding more questions if necessary. Keep drilling down and getting more specific. You may need a few thinking sessions over some time.

"Had I been more thoughtful (and less emotionally impulsive) in the initial decision-making process, I would have made far fewer bad choices and, as a result, my wealth would be many multiples of what it is today . . . and so would yours."

Now you should have some solid facts and ideas of what you want. Let's use our earlier example about moving cities.

- **Figure out what matters to you**: Use your thinking time to think about what's important for your ideal living situation. Are you looking for a city with great job opportunities in your field? Do you want a place with a vibrant cultural scene, or maybe you're seeking peace and quiet? How about the cost of living, weather, or proximity to family and friends? Rate how important each is. I suggest using a decision matrix. You put all of those criteria for the various choices you have. You can then rate the importance of each criterion. Tally those up into a score.

Decision matrix

Using a decision matrix can help to take the emotions out of a decision. It will also give you a more balanced perspective.

Begin by listing the options to choose from. Next add what criteria are important to you. Then rate their importance. Now you can add a score from 1 - 5 on those criteria. Each will add up to a score based on the weight. Make sure you adjust and think about this a few times as your perspective will shift. Don't do it in one go.

Come back to it and think hard about it. You can find a template of this decision matrix on my website.

	A	B Location	C Price	D Area	E Stability	F Final Weight
2	Weight	2.00	2.00	1.00	1.00	
3	HOUSE 1	4	4	5	3	24
4	HOUSE 2	1	5	3	5	20
5		why is location important?	why is price important?	why is area important?	why is stability important?	
6	Add notes about what this means to you					0

- **Research your options**: Now you start looking up cities that might match your criteria. Maybe you're eyeing a bustling metropolis for its job market, a cozy small town for its community feel, or a sunny coastal city for its beach vibes. Rate the quality of each option and how it meets your criteria of what's important.

- **Compare the pros and cons**: Make a list of your top city choices and compare them side by side. How does each city stack up in terms of job opportunities, cost of living, lifestyle, and the other factors you've identified as important? Get the facts for all of the options. Use a decision matrix tool to rate them. I have included one on my list at the end of this book.

- **Consider your long-term goals**: Think about where you see yourself in the next 5 to 10 years. Does one of these cities seem like a place where you could achieve those goals? Maybe one city has better schools, if you're planning on starting a family, or another has a thriving industry related to your career ambitions. It's not just about the immediate move but also about the chain of events that move will set off. Think about the ripple effects. It also combines probabilistic thinking. Since you can't truly know, think in terms of likelihoods and odds. It's recognizing that few things are certain, but you can play the odds to make better choices. This mindset is helpful in making decisions under uncertainty, allowing you to weigh risks and benefits more effectively.

- **Fear setting:** When we make a decision, many of us spiral into overthinking: what if this and what if that? Gaining clarity on all the risks involved with a decision is an effective way to move forward. Getting them out in the open makes us understand that it's not so bad and we can actually grow and overcome many perceived challenges. You should also write about the benefits you will gain from each situation. A helpful way to deal with this is the fear-setting exercise by Tim Ferris. Open up a spreadsheet or divide a piece of paper into three columns. Write the following.
    - Column 1: write down all the "what-ifs" that you're worried about happening.
    - Column 2: write down how likely you think it is that each what-if could come true. Do this on a scale of 1 to 5.

- Column 3: write down what you would do if it did happen.
  - Realize that when bad things happen, there is usually a solution. Apart from death, most stuff can be resolved.
- **Visit if possible**: If you can, visit your top city choices. There's nothing like experiencing a place firsthand to see whether it feels right. Pay attention to how you feel walking the streets, eating in local restaurants, and imagining your life there.
- **Make your decision**: Armed with all this information and your personal impressions, decide which city aligns best with your needs, desires, and future plans. It's not just about the practicalities; it's also about where you can see yourself truly happy and thriving. Once you've made your choice, start planning your move. In our example of moving cities, it involves looking for a place to live, figuring out job opportunities, and planning the logistics of moving. Choosing where to live is a significant decision that impacts your lifestyle, career, social life, and overall happiness. By using rational optimization, you're thoughtfully considering all aspects

to make the best choice for you and your future.

"Once the Choice is Made, Do Not Look Back, Do Not Second-Guess Your Decisions." - *Muhammad Ali*

Lastly, remember that we all make mistakes. From those, we can learn or win. With this in mind, understand that your goal should not be perfection. That's just not possible. Instead, work on reducing blind spots. The focus should not be on intelligence but rather on not being stupid.

In short, life's too short to get hung up on finding the perfect solution for everything. Aim for "good enough," keep moving, and focus on what's in front of you. That's how you get things done and keep your sanity intact.

"Go to bed smarter than when you woke up." - *Charlie Munger*

CHALLENGE 8

Thinking time.

Now it's time to think! I want you to schedule three one-hour thinking sessions this week. Do it when you're not too tired and you have the time clear. Plan ahead what you're going to think about. It should be challenges you want to overcome or goals you want to achieve.

Find a quiet place to sit and be still. Put a notepad and pen next to you. At the top of the page, write a question related to solving the challenge or achieving the goal.

Turn off all devices and set a timer for forty-five minutes. Begin thinking. If your mind wanders, keep coming back to the question. Write down any ideas you have that are useful. When the timer goes off, spend fifteen minutes organizing your notes.

You can keep coming back to certain thinking topics with new angles and questions. Thinking constructively is a game changer, and I hope it helps you improve your life.

CHAPTER 8
LETTING GO

In a quest for inner peace, the ancient Stoics handed down a wisdom as relevant today as it was in their time. They organized life into two categories: what we can control and what we cannot control. This distinction lays the foundation for a profound practice: Letting go. By focusing our energies on what is within our control and releasing our grip on what isn't, we pave the way to a life marked by tranquility and contentment.

Letting go is a practice of mindful release that opens us up to the richness of life. It teaches us to distinguish between what demands our energy and what requires our release. That which we can control and that which we cannot. This practice is not about losing ourselves but about finding a deeper connection to the essence of who we are, leading us to a place of inner peace.

As you already know, your thoughts keep generating more thoughts in a continuous loop. It is the mind's way of trying to make sense of our feelings. When we feel something, our mind tries to come up with reasons for those feelings. To do so, it creates thoughts. However, the true cause of our feelings isn't the thoughts or things happening around us, but rather a buildup of pressure or energy within us that needs to be released. The thoughts and external happenings are just the surface explanations our mind invents. They are not the real root of our feelings.

Dr. David R. Hawkins, in his work on letting go, echoes a timeless truth. The essence of what we seek externally resides within us. Success, health, and happiness are not contingent on external circumstances but are part of our intrinsic human nature. By turning our gaze inward, we can embark on a journey of discovery to find our true potential. Or as many self-help gurus would say, to become the best version of ourselves.

Yet, achieving this state of inner harmony requires us to confront and release the blocks that hinder our path. The overthinking mind, the one holding us prisoner to fears, expectations, preconceived notions, and stress that clouds our true selves. We must let go of it all by surrendering to it. Hawkins guides us through this pathway of surrender, teaching us that inner peace is not found in holding tightly onto our desires but in the release.

The art of letting go

Surrender is the art of letting go, of releasing the tight grip we hold on to our desires, fears, expectations, and overthinking. It is the realization that, despite our best efforts, there are forces at play larger than ourselves: currents in the river of life that can carry us to unforeseen destinations if we only let them; overthinking that clouds our judgment and life experience. It's about trusting the process, understanding that sometimes, the path to true fulfillment and happiness requires us to stop swimming against the tide and instead, float, allowing the waters to guide us.

Consider the mightiest of trees, standing tall and proud in the forest. Even in the face of the fiercest storms, it knows when to bend, understanding that in flexibility, there is survival. The power of surrender is much the same; it's recognizing when to fight and when to adapt, knowing that sometimes, our greatest victories come not from conquering every battle but in choosing which battles are worth the fight.

The narrative of life is filled with complexity and nuance, much like the journey of a leaf adrift in the autumn wind. There is strength in surrender, in the graceful dance with the forces that move us. Surrender is not about giving up, but giving in to the moment, fully and without reservation. In surrender, there is a profound power. The power to experience life to its fullest. To appreciate the beauty of life and to find a sense of peace amidst the chaos, even when the destination remains unseen. In surrender, we find room to breathe, to grow, and to open ourselves to new possibilities. Like the seed that falls to the ground, surrendering to the darkness of the soil. In this act of letting go, we find the potential for new life, for transformation and rebirth.

As Hawkins suggests, this silent surrender is not a passive act but a powerful step toward achieving inner peace and fulfillment. So, let us learn from the leaf and the tree, from the ebb and flow of the tides, and embrace the power of surrender. For in the act of letting go, we might just find everything we've been searching for, not by seizing it, but by allowing it to unfold, beautifully and naturally, in its own time and in its own way.

How to let go

Letting go begins with self-awareness. When you catch yourself overthinking, allow those thoughts to come up and run their course. Don't try to change the thoughts or do anything about them. Just be there with them. Notice that you might have fear, guilt, and shame over the feelings coming up. Let go of those reactions and embrace the feeling. Ignore any thoughts; just focus on the feeling itself and not the thoughts. Simply see it as a feeling, and surrender all efforts to modify it in any way. Any resistance to it will just keep the feeling going. Once you give up resistance to it, you will shift yourself to the next feeling. One that is to be accompanied by a lighter sensation. This is the process of letting go, and it will cause the energy behind those initial feelings to dissipate. It's that simple. :) Just let each one come up and run its course without wanting to do anything about it.

In some cases, the feelings of negativity may be so strong that they continue to return. That means there is still more to be surrendered. Over the years, we've stuffed down these feelings in our lives, and that energy is deeply manifested within ourselves. When it comes up, we have to acknowledge it and let it go. In the process of continually letting go, we're moving toward freedom. Only when we can acknowledge the negativity that we've inherited from the human condition will we have the possibility of surrendering and being free of it. We simply need to be willing to acknowledge and accept that part of our human experience. By accepting it, we can transcend it.

"The major requirement for the journey is a willingness to let go of the attachment to your current experience of life."

Understand, as the feelings come and go, you are not the feelings, but you are witnessing them. When you stop to identify with your mind, you become more aware of this changelessness within you; you'll start to identify with that level of consciousness. That's when you get closer and closer to your real self and connected with the universe. Once, you were the victim of your feelings; now you see they are not you. They are merely created by the ego, a collection of the mind that is mistakenly being thought of as essential for survival.

The more you practice letting go, the more you'll notice how your negative feelings are intricately linked with basic survival mechanisms. It's human nature to feel fear and to protect ourselves in a bid for survival. The letting go technique acknowledges this and short circuits them. When we surrender our feelings, it lets go of the emotions. We become freer.

When we are free, we have let go of attachments and we can enjoy the present moment. There is no dependence on anyone or anything outside of ourselves. Inner fulfillment becomes our state. This concept closely relates to the teaching of Buddha to avoid attachments, in addition to the teachings of Jesus Christ to "be in the world but not of it."

Letting go is a simple thing that we can do every day. There is no dogma or belief system. You don't need to pray or bow down to anyone. Everything you need is within you. "The truth shall set you free" and "the kingdom of God is within you." So, realize that it's in your power to let go, in any place, and with any event. Liberation from our minds is an amazing thing. You can be free from overthinking. Then you are in charge of where to direct your thoughts. You are no longer at the mercy of the world and your reactions to it. It is freedom from overthinking.

Shift your thoughts

In letting go, we can begin to build a better mindset. One that is free from overthinking. Understand that you must take full responsibility for your mind. Positive thoughts and a great mindset won't just appear. You have to curate them.

"One of the most significant findings in psychology in the last twenty years is that

individuals can choose the way they think." - Martin Seligman

Tony Robbins is renowned as one of the leading figures in the self-improvement sector. He advocates a powerful technique that involves reshaping the narratives we construct about our lives. Consider a scenario in which your date is running twenty minutes late without responding to your texts. You have the option to interpret this situation in various ways, such as assuming the person will not arrive or believing they've been held up.

Take another case: imagine your manager hasn't replied to your email regarding a possible salary increase. You might think that you won't get the raise. But perhaps your boss simply hasn't had the chance to respond yet.

The essence of Tony Robbins' advice is to consciously alter your narratives to foster a more optimistic outlook, thereby reducing tendencies toward panic, anxiety, and excessive worry. By managing the stories, you tell yourself, you can significantly impact your mental well-being. Ask yourself whether your internal narratives are empowering or detrimental. Do you often think:

"I'm prone to worrying too much," or

"I'm not capable enough"?

To transform these limiting beliefs, start by identifying them, especially during challenging times. Jot down your initial reactions to such situations and look for any recurring patterns. Then, actively work on crafting more positive and supportive narratives. Changing your personal story can profoundly influence your life's trajectory for the better. Keep up the positive self-talk!

Affirmations are another great tool for this purpose. However, many people don't use them properly. As a result, they can have the wrong effect and give people a feeling of low self-worth. The main reason is that people often use unrealistic affirmations that are beyond their current scope of reality. For example, if your bank balance is near zero and you tell yourself that you're a billionaire, it's going to be very hard to believe. Start smaller and build up the levels. For example, you could say, "I am on the pathway to wealth," or "I am making six grand a month." Simply make them more believable.

Go ahead and write down a bunch of empowering and believable affirmations to steer you in the right direction. Say them to yourself all day, every day. I often do this when I'm struggling to do a workout or something challenging. When the mental noise is strong, I use a mantra. For example, "hard work, dedication" or "I can do this" or "powerful, strong." Choose whatever you feel is empowering. Repeat it over and over in your mind. Do it fast, do it slow. Just keep spamming it into your mind, and it will kick out those thoughts that push you down. If you're currently dissatisfied with your life or self-perception, it's important to counteract negative thoughts with positive affirmations and adopt a mindset focused on growth and self-improvement. Moreover, adjusting your physical posture to reflect confidence and ceasing the comparison of your journey to others are practical steps toward nurturing a more positive self-view.

Gratitude

A person who is more grateful for their life manifests better thoughts and, in turn, a better life. Overall, your life will be more productive and happier. Start to pay attention to all the things you are grateful for. From the small to the big. The wind in the trees, the quiet at night, a comfy chair, a roof over your head, good health, friends, and so on.

Start and end your days on a note of gratitude. Think about those things you're grateful for before you sleep. Write whatever you're grateful for when you wake up. Practice it all day. The more gratitude you cultivate, the happier your life will be and the less stressed you'll be. Focus on your blessings.

Self-esteem

People who enjoy good health and happiness often possess a robust sense of self-esteem. They tend to engage in less overthinking and experience a higher quality of life. Self-esteem is a psychological concept that refers to one's self-assessment of worth. Simply put, it measures how much an individual appreciates themselves. Throughout our lives, self-esteem can vary significantly, influenced by factors such as health, genetics, socioeconomic status, and the people we surround ourselves with.

Our subconscious mind meticulously records all our actions, contributing to the formation of our self-esteem. Engaging in dishonest behaviors such as lying, cheating, and stealing erodes trust. Worst of all, it damages the trust we have in ourselves, which can significantly increase anxiety, worry, and negativity. Such actions, stored in our subconscious, can shape our behavior in detrimental ways over time. To avoid this, it's crucial to embody the values we advocate, which, in turn, fosters integrity and self-respect. Maintaining unwavering integrity in all aspects of life, including financial responsibilities, is a principle that can lead to peace of mind. This level of honesty can also significantly reduce overthinking. Remember, each person's path is unique, and focusing on your own growth and values is key to developing a stronger sense of self-esteem.

Embracing simplicity

As we wrap up this chapter on letting go, it's clear that the journey toward inner peace isn't about grand gestures or radical changes overnight. It's about the small steps we take every day, the moments we choose to release rather than cling to, and the decisions we make to focus on what truly matters.

Letting go isn't a one-time act; it's a practice we weave into the fabric of our daily lives. It's in the deep breath we take when frustration mounts, the gentle reminder to ourselves that not everything requires our reaction, and the quiet acceptance of life's ebb and flow. It's in the recognition that, while we can't control every aspect of our existence, we can decide where to invest our energy and attention.

Think of letting go as decluttering the mind. Just as we periodically clean out our living spaces, removing what no longer serves us to make room for what does, so too must we clear our mental landscapes. It involves recognizing the thoughts, feelings, and beliefs that have overstayed their welcome and gently, but firmly, showing them the door.

This doesn't mean ignoring our emotions or pretending they don't exist. On the contrary, it's about acknowledging them, understanding their origins, and then choosing not to let them dictate our actions. It's about saying, "I see you, I hear you, but I choose not to be swayed by you."

As we move forward, let's carry with us the simple yet profound lessons of letting go. Let's make it a habit to pause and ask ourselves whether what we're holding onto is worth the space it occupies in our hearts and minds. Let's commit to releasing the need for certainty and control, embracing instead the beauty of uncertainty and the freedom it brings.

Remember, the journey of letting go is uniquely yours. There's no right or wrong way to do it, only your way. And with each step, each release, you'll find yourself moving closer to the peace and contentment you've been seeking. Not because you've found the secret to a perfect life, but because you've discovered the strength and resilience within yourself to navigate life's ups and downs with grace.

CHALLENGE 9

Are there any persistent thoughts that you have been experiencing recently? The next time they come up, let them happen. Don't try to distract yourself or make up something that urgently needs to be done. Just sit still and allow them to play out in your mind. Observe it all. Let those feelings come up and immerse yourself in them. When they play out, notice how not resisting eventually reduces their intensity.

Let go and feel the release.

____

____

____

____

____

____

____

____

CONCLUSION

Success is a journey on which you will be met with many ups and downs. Many of those will be of your own making. In that regard, overthinking is often the biggest hurdle to overcome. We've seen how it can wreak havoc in our lives. We've seen how it's holding us back. You don't need me to give you examples of it because I'm sure you know it all too well.

The main message I gave at the start of this book was **Most people are afraid to think.** But everything begins as a thought. We just need the best thoughts. This book has been about redirecting your thinking from destructive overthinking to being constructive or at peace. Being aware of the distractions, diversions, and manipulation that take you away from your purpose.

I began this book by explaining how overthinking happens and how to be aware of the triggers that set it off, from the problems we face inside, due to our human nature, to the problems we face outside, due to the environment, influences, manipulation, and content we face on a daily basis.

To solve this, what I presented in this book were **four pillars** to make your overthinking become constructive or subdued. Now let's summarize those.

- **Finding purpose:** In order to reduce our overthinking, we first need to find a purpose for living. Purpose comes from the meaning we attribute to the things we do. Find more meaning and you will think less.
- **Lifestyle:** Building a wholesome lifestyle follows on from finding purpose. With a purpose-driven life, we can start to build a meaningful and fulfilling lifestyle. Fill your life up with wonderful, healthy, fulfilling living.
- **Mindfulness:** This teaches us to enjoy life right now. The present moment is all we have. It also reveals the problem with thought identification and teaches us that we are not our thoughts.
- **Letting go:** When unhelpful thoughts come up, we don't attach ourselves to them. We simply let them come up and pass us by. This frees us from overthinking.

With the knowledge and lessons you have found in this book, you can bring more stillness, clarity, and inner peace into your life. Furthermore, you will be able to make better decisions. The result is naturally going to be a better quality of life. One which you are gaining control over. A life of meaning.

Each chapter in this book has its own key

takeaways. Read it again as you progress in life. You don't necessarily need to read the book all the way through. I suggest you dip in now and then. Keep re-reading it. As your life moves forward, you will change. When you read this book again, some things will stand out more, and you will keep growing as a result.

Gandhi's call to "be the change you want to see in the world" is not just a rallying cry for external activism but a reminder of the power of personal transformation. Our inner work does not exist in a vacuum; it ripples outward, influencing the world in ways both subtle and profound. As we work on improving ourselves, the effects ripple out into the outside world.

Work on being a better person.

Use the tools in this book to do that. When you clear away the dark clouds of overthinking, the real you can emerge. I wish the best for you.

And if you enjoyed this book, please review it and share it.

Best wishes

Tommy Swindali

REFERENCES

1.   Smith, j. M., & alloy, l. B. (2009). A roadmap to rumination: a review of the definition, assessment, and conceptualization of this multifaceted construct. Clinical psychology review, 29(2), 116–128. Https://doi.org/10.1016/j.cpr.2008.10.003

2.   Dobelli, r. (2014). The art of thinking clearly. Harper collins.

3. 6 tips to stop overthinking. (n.d.). Https://www.psychologytoday.com/us/blog/what-mentally-strong-people-dont-do/201602/6-tips-stop-overthinking

4.   Eklof, k., & eklof, k. (2020, june 18). What happens to your body when you overthink? Edexec. Supporting business and financial excellence in schools and academies. Https://edexec.co.uk/what-happens-to-your-body-when-you-overthink/

5.   Nasar, s. (2012). A beautiful mind. Faber & faber.

6.   Michl, l. C., mclaughlin, k. A., shepherd, k., & nolen-hoeksema, s. (2013). Rumination as a mechanism linking stressful life events to symptoms of depression and anxiety: longitudinal evidence in early adolescents and adults. Journal of abnormal psychology, 122(2), 339–352. Https://doi.org/10.1037/a0031994

7.   Any anxiety disorder. (n.d.). National institute of mental health (nimh). Https://www.nimh.nih.gov/health/statistics/any-anxiety-disorder

8.   Qasim, t. B., sahar, a., nihal, t., & bashir, a. (2022). The effect of overthinking on mental health: a case study from university students in multan district. Review of applied management and social sciences, 5(2), 255–262. Https://doi.org/10.47067/ramss.v5i2.233

9.   Edblad, p. (2019). The decision-making blueprint: a simple guide to better choices in life and work.

10. Amaha. (n.d.). How to overcome overthinking. Amaha. Https://www.amahahealth.com/blog/science-behind-overthinking/

11. Ciesla, j. A., dickson, k. S., anderson, n. L., & neal, d. J. (2011). Negative repetitive thought and college drinking: angry rumination, depressive rumination, co-rumination, and worry. Cognitive therapy and research, 35(2), 142–150. Https://doi.org/10.1007/s10608-011-9355-1

12. Homeostasis. Nih. (n.d.). Https://www.ncbi.nlm.nih.gov/pmc/articles/pmc7076167/

13. Dodsworth, l., & fagan, p. (2023). Free your mind: the new world of manipulation and how to resist it. Harpercollins uk.

14. Kruglanski, a. (2023). Uncertain: how to turn your biggest fear into your greatest power. Random house.

15. Zahariades, d. (2021). How to make better decisions: 14 smart tactics for curbing your biases, managing your emotions, & making fearless decisions in every area of your life!

16. Tolle, e. (2010). The power of now: a guide to spiritual enlightenment. New world library.

17. Singer, m. A. (2007). The untethered soul: the journey beyond yourself. New harbinger publications.

18. Frankl, v. E. (1992). Man's search for meaning: an introduction to logotherapy. Beacon press (ma).

19. Schopenhauer, a. (2010). The essential schopenhauer: key selections from the world as will and representation and other works. Harper collins.

20. Schwarzenegger, a. (2023). Be useful: seven tools for life. Random house.

21. Carnegie, d. (2019). How to stop worrying & start living.

22. Roberts, d. L. (2023, november 21). Overthinking and rumination – the dark side of thinking our thoughts. Newsbreak original. Https://original.newsbreak.com/@dr-donna-l-roberts-561947/3237547651301-overthinking-and-rumination-the-dark-side-of-thinking-our-thoughts

23. Brain basics: understanding sleep. (n.d.). National institute of neurological disorders and stroke. Https://www.ninds.nih.gov/health-information/public-education/brain-basics/brain-basics-understanding-sleep

24. Taleb, n.n. Antifragile: things that gain from disorder. (2012.). Random house.

25. Seligman, m. (2011). Authentic happiness: using the new positive psychology to realize your potential for lasting fulfillment. Hachette uk.

26. Seligman, m. E. P. (2006). Learned optimism: how to change your mind and your life (reprint ed.). Vintage.

27. Sara lazar, ph.d.: how meditation changes the structure of the brain. (n.d.). Massachusetts general hospital. Https://www.massgeneral.org/charged/episodes/sara-lazar

28. Hölzel, b. K., carmody, j., vangel, m., congleton, c., yerramsetti, s. M., gard, t., & lazar, s. W. (2011). Mindfulness practice leads to increases in regional brain gray matter density. Psychiatry research: neuroimaging, 191(1), 36–43. Https://doi.org/10.1016/j.pscychresns.2010.08.006

29. Keng, s., smoski, m. J., & robins, c. J. (2011). Effects of mindfulness on psychological health: a review of empirical studies. Clinical psychology review, 31(6), 1041–1056. Https://doi.org/10.1016/j.cpr.2011.04.006

30. Viljoen, e. (2013). The power of meditation: an ancient technique to access your inner power. Penguin.

31. Jean buridan's logic: the treatise on supposition the treatise on consequences. (2012). Springer science & business media.

32. Clarke, j. (2023, november 27). What is analysis paralysis? Verywell mind. Https://www.verywellmind.com/what-is-analysis-paralysis-5223790

33. Kahneman, d. (2011). Thinking, fast and slow. Penguin uk.

34. Schwartz, d. J. (2016). The magic of thinking big. Random house.

35. Cunningham, k. J. (2017). The road less stupid: advice from the chairman of the board.

36. Ferriss, t. (2007). The 4-hour workweek: escape 9-5, live anywhere, and join the new rich. Crown archetype.

37. Hawkins, d. R., md ph.d. (2014). Letting go: the pathway of surrender. Hay house, inc.

38. Robbins, a. (1999). Unleash the power within: personal coaching to transform your life. Simon & schuster audio/nightingale-conant.

39. Seneca, l. A., & campbell, r. (1969). Letters from a stoic. (penguin classics) (reprint ed.). Penguin books.

40. Krockow, e.m., ph.d. The dangers of overthinking. (2023).

41. How did the universe begin? (n.d.). American museum of natural history. Https://www.amnh.org/explore/ology/astronomy/how-did-the-universe-begin

FREE GIFT

Greetings!

First of all, I want to thank you for reading my books. I aim to create the very best books for my readers.

Now I invite you to join my exclusive list. As a subscriber, you will receive a free gift, weekly tips, free giveaways, discounts, and so much more.

<u>All of this is 100% free with no strings attached.</u>

To claim your bonus, simply head to the link below or scan the QR code.

https://www.subscribepage. com/swindali

www.ingramcontent.com/pod-product-compliance
Lightning Source LLC
Chambersburg PA
CBHW071947150726
47999CB00001B/345